FROM MY
BRAIN
TO YOUR
EYES

Let Nothing Defeat You

R.J. Edwards

ISBN 978-1-54396-307-6

CONTENTS

LOVE AND AFFECTION—1

PAIN AND REGRET—25

FANTASY—43

FORGIVENESS AND RECONCILATION—165

RESPECT AND LOYALTY—169

FORWARD

Inspired by his own experiences with abuse, betrayal, love, growth and physical and mental breakdown, R.J. Edwards presents his unique and transcendent poem collection, From My Brain to Your Eyes.

I have known R.J. for over fifteen years-in fact I've seen him grow through adversity and self-growth. Over the years, we've talked privately about our experiences and his ambitions today, and spending time with him and his family. Words can't express how therapeutic it has been to see R.J not only develop his voice but to develop a new love of poetry. Edwards has tackled poetry as it was the fourth quarter in the game. He was up early reading daily other authors, and doing extensive research, and self- reflection to develop his strategy.

I've seen him stand before audiences large and small. I've come to know this dynamic, fearless man so well that I count him as my friend. I reveal our own personal friendship in these pages because I want you, to know firsthand what a phenomenal giving human being he is "in my eyes." In all of my countless hours with him, his spirit always- and I mean always shines light that captures everyone within its boundaries.

The book's title is explained in the first pages—his reference to women, love, pain, and loneliness is just the beginning of R.J Edwards grabbing hold of his voice and diminishing the stigma of the silent athlete. This recurrent theme provides a strong framework for Edwards to branch out from, all the while reinforcing his message of intense self-exploration. As a result, From My Brain to Your Eyes is more than a collection of poems - it is a stunning, fully coherent whole story of a man's emotions and thoughts.

Memoir-type poems about love or challenges are common, but Edwards works serve as excellent examples that also elevate the convention. Personal and unguarded, he forms an intimate connection through his poems while exploring metaphors and parallel stories through allusions and the abundant use of music and pop culture inferences. These devices are integral to the poems, making Edwards poetic universe larger and more inclusive by invoking the universal human experience, not just his own. This is true whether Edwards poems parallel a thought or quote by another, or artfully redirect original meaning.

Several of the poems were written for specific occasions: relationships, friendship, career, and emotions. Each captures the essence of those moments in a way that's both personal and universal, for a man in America.

To me, R.J. went through his life not sharing all the details. This book is the start of him sharing the details of his life one poem at a time. More than that, he is a living example, of what we can all accomplish by taking the first step. I am beyond proud of this father, son, brother, athlete, entrepreneur, and now poet truly living his dreams.

I am honored to write these few words, you the reader are about to immense yourself in. I assure you, that you'll be moved and interested to read every stanza.

R.J. is a poet armed with life experience and craft, two weapons that he brings to bear with full force in this book: From My Brain to Your Eyes.

-Michelle Rankine

LOVE AND AFFECTION

One
By: R.J. Edwards

If I can't have one,

I shall love none.

If I want one,

Why can't I have her who turns me on?

She wants me,

And I want her.

I desire to make her smile,

Even if it is just for a little while.

But the time has change once again.

What was once there has faded all away as if it were a sin.

If I can't love one

I shall love none.

Feelings
By: R.J. Edwards

My feelings for you are as high as these ceilings.

But they can also be as low as someone drilling.

Why do I keep going back and forth with you?

To be honest and speak the truth,

I really don't have a clue.

Maybe because in this life, I'll only come across a chosen few.

But that shouldn't be my excuse.

To be used and taking all types of verbal abuse,

I think it's time for me to step away from this situation and these feelings.

To start some major healing,

For through our dealings,

My wounds have done nothing but major spilling.

Before I'm just a shell of a man.

I'll just have to leave you speaking to the hand.

I'm no longer gonna stand here like a dumb man.

To be mistreated and abuse like I got a short attention span.

I'll let you save up for the next man.

Love
By: R.J. Edwards

Never in a million years would I thought I'd be here

Life turned upside down yet it's still turning around

Been planning for it all my life but it's still nowhere to be found

So high in the air yet I'm here stuck on the ground.

How can I be so passionate about you, but you lead me astray?

I love things black and white, but you live in the grey

Why do you choose to treat me as a clown when I know you get around?

Every time someone loses you, they find a frown
and for months they can't put it down.

You smell so good yet stink very bad especially when you leave people sad

My day is near I can feel it coming

I can even hear the little drummers drumming

Please don't fill my heart with fear as if I'm walking off a pier

Let my love catch me as to say I am here

For I've been looking for her for years.

Love
By: R.J. Edwards

Roots deeper than the uncharted parts of the sea

Know that can't no one break what is meant to be

The strength we show together has never been seen

Our foundation starts with you and me.

King and Queen, it's how we start our family tree

Heirs to the throne will be more than three

We're going to build an empire for the entire world to see

Believing in one another is the true key

I know without you there is no me.

Love
By: R.J. Edwards

Greatness needs greatness to become phenomenal.

Anything less you might just become nominal.

Being phenomenal takes time, effort and commitment.

Not holding grudges and being resistant.

Change is one thing that's inevitable.

Don't make decisions that are very regrettable.

Look at things differently to get better results.

Or your love life might be a crime scene outlined in chalk.

I know changing your views on things is a massive thing

But what do you really have to lose?

Besides being in this life without the number one thing

Love.

Polyamory
By: R.J. Edwards

If you are looking for a traditional relationship.

I ain't it.

I got too much love for it period.

Don't think you're going to get with me and change me.

That'll be a lost cause like when guys say pause after a sentence.

I'm not doing this to keep my distance or from a commitment.

I'm doing this because this is who I am

I love Keisha Tammy and Pam.

Being with one woman for the rest of my life.

Would be like choosing to eat spam for the rest of my life.

I love being in the company of beautiful women.

So how could I choose just one.

When there's so many

If I can have one, shouldn't I have plenty?

You think I'm just saying that because I'm empty?

I'm full of love and I want it to catch all the single
ladies in my glove to show them true love.

You say how can I have so much love to give

Life was hard, and I didn't know what love was.

Now that I know I have a lot to give

I just really want to live.

With no restrictions and boundaries

With loving people and women all around me.

We

By: R.J. Edwards

I know our love will cause a lot of heads to turn and faces to frown up.

As our love doesn't follow the rules of society.

As they say true love is between two not three.

If that was true, wouldn't everyone be married living happily ever after?

Who really has the clues?

To not catching the blues.

You see, society will have you second guessing every action.

To keep you on their agenda and giving you no satisfaction,

It's a new time,

I got two beautiful Queens with me.

Together we're going to show the power of three,

No nights alone

Always being held and warm

Don't get mad and try to ring a jealousy alarm

Just find yourself someone or ones that make you always feel at home

Since we are grown, we used our minds and turned a house into home.

No matter if you have a bone to pick with how
we are choosing to live our lives.

We're happy and enjoying our life.

Don't you see we can careless about your strife
in what you consider as right?

We hope through us you see the light.

For then your future could be as bright.

Love
By: R.J. Edwards

Love is so....

Fragile,

Soft,

And Unpredictable.

So how is it so....

Strong,

Powerful,

And Conquering

All at the same time?

Love is all these things

As it is formless.

It takes on the character

Of the one who holds it.

Don't let Love lead you

Be the Leader of love.

Forgotten Ones
By: R.J. Edwards

I'm so through with girls that without me would be on section eight.

I tried to show them that there's more to life and it could be great.

Why did I do that?

Just turns out it made them into a bigger basket case.

Beautiful as can be,

Pretty face,

Nice little body,

And petite.

But inside like Rumpke

Man, did they fool me?

Empty
By: R.J. Edwards

When I've searched everywhere for you and
can't find you, I just feel so empty.

I know you don't believe me.

Look how my sweat has stained my clothes as I searched for you.

I'm just sitting here at the bar drinking my
Rémy, wishing I could find my boo.

I've worked so hard to build this life for two.

Only to find out that it'll be no breakthrough.

I think to myself,

What should I do to fill this void?

Should I now treat every woman that I meet like my little toy?

Wouldn't that be wrong of me?

Only if I could see the end of each relationship.

Leaving them sad and lonely, wishing they had never met me and shit.

I'm not a bad guy, I just got a different focus.

I'm looking for that one that will get me feeling to feeling hopeless

She can fill this empty fuel tank called my heart.

Show me why she'll always be legions apart.

From all the other girls I've dated,

Who had me so damn frustrated.

Making me smile on my worst days,

For she knows I love the little games she plays.

I'll never stop searching for you as you are my queen.

I need you with me in this movie as the world is our screen.

We must show everyone what true love is all about.

For when they find their mate they'll never doubt.

For life is not always pretty.

But we loved each other when we didn't have any penny.

Affection
By: R.J. Edwards

I love showing you my affection.

With your soul, it deserves nothing but perfection.

In your Beauty, I see such wonderful things.

I just look at you like an angel that's about to sprout wings.

Your style and grace,

Can brighten up anyplace.

Like a hundred flowers on a mantle in a pretty vase.

I'm glad that I have the honor of showering you with my affection.

I don't want to be the reason for us having a disconnection.

I love all that you are and will become.

Since I know where this beautiful flower has blossomed from,

I will let nothing get in the way of my love for you.

Since the first time I laid eyes on you,

I knew I was going to make you my boo.

Who knew it would all come true.

Trying to say the first thing to you,

I had no clue.

I had courage in my heart and that was my start.

Now it was time for my body to do its part.

As I introduced myself, I saw the glimmer in your eye.

You were happy I came over to say hi.

I wanted to make you feel how you made me
feel like I was the luckiest guy.

While talking in the night, I said I was going to fly you through the sky.

Our future is planned since I'm now your man.

Just wait in a couple of months you'll have a band on your hand.

I knew when I saw you, you would be mine.

Just to show you it wasn't a line,

I had to let you see for yourself all in due time.

Now you're so beautiful walking down the aisle to me.

As we are now in a place where we both agreed we wanted to be.

I love you with all my heart.

I think it's cool I knew that from the very start.

Loving you is easy because you are a wonderful piece of art.

I'm just glad we came together and now let's never be apart.

Doubt
By: R.J. Edwards

You doubted my love for you.

Was it because you didn't receive the official title of being my main boo?

I took you on trips and even made a fantasy come true.

But you still doubted me now ain't that just rude.

I wanted to be your dude and take you on more trips even a cruise.

So that we could sail the seas while checking out some crazy views.

But you wanted to doubt me thinking I was only here to abuse you.

I thought through my actions I showed you
that I would never misuse you.

I guess I didn't make it clear enough that I loved you and all that you do

Now I'm out here once again looking for a love that is true.

Light
By: R.J. Edwards

You light my way on my darkest day.

For without you I know I would go astray.

I love to make you smile for that lights up my day.

Your love for me keeps me at bay.

I was once told I would be nothing.

But once you came into my life, I knew I had to be something.

For you gave me a foundation something I could build upon.

Now here's a house and yard with your own little pond.

People don't understand why I'm so fond of you.

For they did not see the transition you helped me through.

I'll always work to be your provider and protector.

Through hell and high water for you my angel
I'll be your everlasting shelter.

Love
By: R.J. Edwards

Why have you always evaded me?

I have been looking for you since I came out of the womb.

Is there a chance I will experience you before I lay at rest in a tomb?

For the people who brought me into this world
never showed me your true meaning.

Since I was a little thing, I never understood your
definition or was shown you any teachings.

Only how I knew who you were was through the T.V.
screen and loud music selling me a dream.

I always wished my parents would come to my rescue,

And give me a clue what I could do with you.

It wasn't till I got finished with my refining stage
that I could truly change the page.

So, now currently I live to show my offspring what you really mean.

But I'm not selling them no dream.

I'm going to show them what this four-letter word mean.

Last
By: R.J. Edwards

If it was only you and I left to build a new empire for our people

Would you join me or never let our people see a sequel?

Through the genocide our worlds got to collide,

Or our people will fall from superiority like the crimson tide.

It wouldn't be due to a ball game,

It'll be because they were slain for what was in their brain.

As they were too dangerous to have around.

They knew before too long they were going to come for that crown.

So, you are telling me that you would pass on extending

our superiority and family tree for someone

that doesn't even look like me.

How could that be?

Are you so brainwashed that you can't see

what you and I were meant to be?

Come spend time with me,

And you'll see the greatness that will accompany you and me,

For many to see and strive to be for they will see all that they can be,

From people who look just like thee.

Rejection
By: R.J. Edwards

After the strong feeling of affection,

You hope a lot of feelings follow besides rejection.

Leaving you sitting there all alone.

Wishing you had a quarter so you could call home.

Nothing you've ever experienced has had your mind in a twist like this.

But you can't do nothing except sit back and reminisce.

Cause, oh boy you got straight diss.

She shook you like a fella that just got done taking a piss.

Just remember you did get to kiss those tender lips,

Even if it was for a bit.

Even though a little while later you feel like
you were dropped off into a pit

I know ain't this some shit.

She is playing with your emotions,

Like she is feeling you and telling people.

Going to start healing you,

All the while peeling you.

Reopening old wounds that you've closed.

When you thought you had an upper hand and
was going to remove her clothes.

Rejection was inevitable in this scenario,

As she wasn't your typical groupie hoe.

Better luck next time with that big ego.

Matter fact just give that thing the heave-ho

If you don't, this is how every relationship will go.

Heart Broken
By: R.J. Edwards

Why is it that women don't get that guys will get to spraying?

When it comes down to another man slaying their woman.

Like guys don't get their feelings hurt.

Let alone that big ego that you just broke.

As you were the token in his eye,

Now you go out getting pounded out by another guy,

While laying next to me telling me boo you're so sweet.

Not knowing you were just on a creep.

But you know what I'm on a creep too.

For when I find him, I'm going to fill him with my tool,

Leaving his body slumped in a pool of his blood,

Having his neighbors thinking this fool did spilt something on his rug.

Not knowing he just got two put in his mug.

For sleeping with another man's wife and ruining his life.

Now he's sent up to the big boy pen to do at least five to ten.

While she's back out on these streets looking for some new meat,

As she like a dog that stays in heat.

Let this be a lesson learned in your life!

Don't ruin your life over a strife with your wife.

What Could Have Been?
By: R.J. Edwards

From the first day I laid my eyes on you,

You always carried yourself as a lady boo.

Even showed other girls how to present themselves too.

Many envied you because of your style and grace,

And I know you sometimes felt out of place.

Coming to a new place full of unknowns and
no one to welcome your new face.

I seen a beautiful girl who strutted to her own beat and pace.

And the woman I know will never see defeat.

I'm getting a little head of myself as I'm speaking of what could have been.

You, the captain of the cheerleading team,

And me the captain of the football team was
supposed to be the match made in heaven.

I guess that only happens in the movies for our story was so different.

You were dating my friends and me dating yours.

The closest we got to each other was the stories
others would implore on us.

I always wondered why we never decided to see
for ourselves what all the fuss was.

But it must have been for the best because none of
those relationships lasted for either of us.

I wouldn't have wanted us to be a bust for I
wouldn't have the friend I do now.

To watch you grow into what you are now it could only make me smile.

Like, wow, look how far we've come, we've totally changed the game.

And you remained totally the same except your last name.

Anticipation
By: R.J. Edwards

It's finally about to happen, me and you spending some alone time

I know you thinking about damn time.

It wasn't all on me

It was plenty of times I was to come see you and make you a smile.

You always left me hanging like an ace with no pair.

I would just fade into the background and stare.

Wonder why you won't allow me to come
lay with you and play in her hair.

Rub on her derrière.

Use her lap as a pillow as I stare into her beautiful eyes
and wonder why it took so long for me to get here.

The truth was revealed that she didn't believe I was that into her.

Even though I sent her those private pictures,

Good Morning texts on a regular and even called from time to time.

Somehow the signal got lost and we never truly connected like a bad call.

Now, the wait is over, and anticipation is at the door.

What's going to happen when my two feet hit
the floor on your side of the door?

As we've never been alone before.

Is the chemistry going to be same?

Are you still going to admire the way of my being?

Or wonder why my phone is on a silent ring?

What does that mean?

So many questions will be answered, and I
wonder if it will all be the same.

After spending time together in a space,

Normally only occupied by you and now you have this
dude there taking up space and all in your face.

Are you ready for that?

Sharing your space and your place?

Not knowing what will happen or is he even a good captain?

We're both willing to take that chance,

As the wait has been long.

As your tired of sitting at home alone listening to love songs.

It's time to see will it all live up to the hype or die by the end of the night.

Anticipation for glory or just another sad story
that is waiting around the corner.

That'll help you put back on that trusty selflove armor.

Know
By: R.J. Edwards

Let me know what?

I know you're not someone to play with.

I'm looking to heal your heart.

Not put it on the wall and throw a dart.

I know it's like a puzzle that's been scattered on the floor.

Just give me time and I'll make it whole once more.

Then you and I can explore the endless possibilities of this world.

That's only if you can trust me once more.

Saying you're down for my actions won't have
me looking like a clown, of course.

For I want to show you I'm down for the cause.

But not looking for an applause.

To show you through actions without assault.

I mean what I say, that one day our home will be the place you lay.

So peaceful till your last days.

Let's come together and mold each other like untampered with clay.

Build each other up to withstand the storms
that are going to come our way.

Put our back together like we are getting jumped in a street fight.

To show the world all this might.

That no matter what comes our way, together we will make it right.

Don't be afraid of me holding your hand at night.

For I plan to be your man,

I'm just letting you know where I stand.

Day Ones
By: R.J. Edwards

It's crazy how we all have children now.

For our journey together started when we were all children ourselves.

Our lives probably haven't went as planned but damn here we stand

Successfully blessed and more than a couple grand on hand.

Far from the days we worked odd jobs and
hustled to get a bob and a quick fade.

Now we get paid and have plenty of spare time to lay up in the shade.

Who would have thought a couple knuckle heads would hit their mark?

We knew we had too and never allowed ourselves to be put in park.

As we achieved one goal after the other,

We were always looking to do another.

I love the people we've become and the way
we didn't allow that to change us.

For when we come together it's as if we are like those kids.

Cracking jokes and telling new stories about our crazy biz.

I love you all from the bottom and top of my heart.

I promise to always make sure you guys are a part of my art.

Icebox
By: R.J. Edwards

Why have you got an icebox where your heart is supposed to be?

Is it because of how guys have mistreated you, abuse you, leaving
you without a clue to who is it you can and should get close to?

I know something about pain as I too have
been run over by the shame train.

Giving someone your all,

Only to turn around and watch as they help you fall on your face

But you knew since the third date that they shouldn't be in your space

It's because of your big heart you overlook the rough start

Ignore the signs that this was just the start to an
unhealthy relationship and wanted to stay on pace

As time went on more lies and deceit followed

You accepted it because you were tired of the chase

Looking for this guy and that guy trying to replace this one
who was all in your face and you knew was a disgrace

The love you've built for him over the years made you blind to the
fact that you've gotten addicted to him like a dope fiend on crack

No matter what he did you could see no wrong.

All it did was keep you singing those same old sad songs.

Until one day you realized you've had enough and
from that point on you were going to act tough

And that my dear is how your icebox was formed.

Though the torment of a love storm.

Check Up
By: R.J. Edwards

Can I come get a checkup as I'm crazy over you?

I know I seem like I got the blues it's just because I'm missing you.

You are the perfect prescription with those pretty eyes, gorgeous smile,
sexy toes, amazing personality, banging body and an outstanding brain.

Only withdrawal is when I can't see you, I go insane.

But you must realize I've never been down this road before.

To have a woman who has it all got me so appalled.

For I never thought I find that in a woman of my generation.

To think I almost let you get away but I'm glad
for the saying better late than never.

For in you I've found a hidden treasure.

This checkup was well needed as I thought my heart had gone cold.

Only to find out it was you I needed to hold.

Now my love can be bold once more until my dying days,
just know I plan to make you happy till I'm old.

To the Limit
By: R.J. Edwards

Limits are meant to be tested right?

How else would one know how deeply they are in love with someone?

How far they would go to receive or get someone attention.

Please don't push the limits too far.

As it can lead to death or heart break.

Which is really both death

For what is life without someone to love?

But a lonely desolate place something like a grave.

Limits are supposed to be tested and even expanded.

For without the Wright Brothers we would still be stranded

Never being able to fly over to Japan.

Don't think you shouldn't expand.

Just don't do it at the expense of the next man.

For it might be you who gets dealt the next short end of the stick.

Leaving you on the end of a brick wall alone staring into the abyss.

Thinking how I got myself into this.

Only if I didn't push so hard.

It wouldn't have ended so swift.

Better or Worse

By: R.J. Edwards

Can you really love me for better or worse?

For you are always screaming at me till your voice goes horse.

You know you are supposed to love me unconditionally.

Instead, it just seems you're just loving me
long enough to get half ironically.

I hope what your actions show just isn't true.

For if they are, I just wouldn't know what to do.

As I loved you through your rampage stage fussing
and fighting like it was you second language.

Why can't you love me through this little baggage?

I know going to the strip club is a bad habit.

But when I come home don't I give it to you like an energized rabbit?

We said for better or worse through any concourse.

But any little disagreement you're ready to grab your keys and purse.

You were not here for the better or worse

You just want me to be a servant while looking
up at you on your high horse.

I loved you through and through and was here to truly bless you.

But here's your ring as I know this is what you wanted me to do.

And I can say with a peaceful mind and spirit we're through.

PAIN AND REGRET

Pain
By: R.J. Edwards

People always wondered what drove me to be me.

It was the pain that drove me to unleash the beast within and
strive for things that people said was one in a million.

Maybe a billion due to that fact I didn't come from a two-parent home.

Everything I did I mostly had to do on my own,

No Father there to drive me to and from practice
and say keep up the excellent job.

Or a mother there to give those cute girls a scare or just a mean glare.

Man, I always use to think life wasn't fair.

I'm going to have grey hair before I become a millionaire.

I could have given up on myself and took the easy route.

By copping myself a pack.

Moving a couple rocks for some stacks.

But I challenged the rule of being a fool,

And went to school.

Not allowing myself to fall into the system.

I figured out a system that would turn a boy into a man.

With more than a few grand.

I thought to myself I must work harder than
everybody else no matter the talent.

I must fight off all the lies, the fears and doubts of
others that were cast upon me to doubt myself.

For, one day I can look at myself in the mirror
and say I did what I ought to do.

And speaking to the kids of my neighborhood you can do it too.

Nightmare
By: R.J. Edwards

It's painful reliving a nightmare every day.

That's the feeling I get every time I see you till this day.

Just to think I used to call you boo.

Damn, what a fool!

I wish I didn't want to see the good in you.

This nightmare could have ended years ago without living a clue.

But, due to my mistake, there's no more flow.

In the way I move.

Now, I'm stuck trying to find my groove

I Should
By: R.J. Edwards

I should have loved you for the million reasons that you gave me

Not the one thing you weren't ready to change

I should have just written it off to youthful age.

Sometimes I feel I'm the one to blame.

Not telling you to just come to me I could be your drug.

Instead I was ok with you going out to the club.

I should have been the only thing you were sipping on.

Not that damn henny bottle.

For once you get that in your system, woman you know you're full throttle

It was my jealousy from not being able to give you that feeling

Which in turn had me willing to leave you with a sad feeling.

I should have just stepped to you like a man.

Said I'm going to stick with our plan.

I shouldn't have abandoned you cause of the little
addiction you were going through

I should have been the Man to see you through.

I should have been there for you.

I should have made all your dreams come true.

I should have been the one for you.

Gone
By: R.J. Edwards

What can I do to have you back in my life?

Do I have to let you know everything is going to be alright?

Do you feel that I'm just talking?

Is that why you keep walking?

What do I have to do to stop you from giving me the run around?

Do I have to put one knee on the ground?

Please, just tell me.

For I can't let this be.

I want another chance to show you what you mean to me.

If not tell me the truth and put me out of my misery.

Fumble
By: R.J. Edwards

What happens if I fumble your heart?

Because you always told me we'd never be apart.

Can you forgive me for my infidelities?

It wasn't you it was me always needing two or three.

Not realizing I had the one and only Queen Bee.

But don't act like that towards me,

Because I was the only one willing to get down on one knee.

To turn the Miss into a Mrs.

Now you are trying to dismiss me for a little foolery.

I told you I wasn't perfect and don't put me on a pedestal.

Because this is love and it can have us all fooled.

Please don't be rude and move on to the next dude.

True I fumbled your heart and that's the real issue

Baby here's some tissue.

And from this day on this will never be an issue.

This is my promise to you.

Nowhere
By: R.J. Edwards

Where did you come from because I'm sure I gave up on this love thing?

I had no plans to explore that anymore.

My heart has been shattered more than a broken glass.

Let down more than the American Flag.

So how could I brag on you?

The last time I felt you, I was just becoming a teen.

And I felt life was so green and not this dark and gloomy thing.

How are you going to change my outlook by coming out of nowhere?

You don't know me or what I've been through

Woman I don't think you even have a clue of what I've truly been through

I've been used and abused more than a used tissue

I know I know this is the same blues you are used to

The same song and dance guys groove to right before they lose you

Yes, I am too good for you.

Listen I'm here to see you through to the other side

That part you thought died

I'm the ocean and this here is a love tide.

Now grab your inner tube and come along for the ride.

I'm going to give you all you've ever imagined.

It's going to be real not a cheap thrill.

Hold on tight because mama is going to make everything right,

For you must no longer put up a fight.

I know I came out of nowhere,

Just know with me around, love will always be just right.

Should Have
By: R.J. Edwards

I should have kept my life simple

I should have never talk to you

I should have kept my goodies to myself

I should have made better decisions

I should have never loved you

Cold Hearted
By: R.J. Edwards

There was a day in which I was so in love with you

Sadly, to say those days are no more.

For those lies you've told destroyed all we had and more.

Nothing you could think of doing that will ever
restore the feelings I once had for you.

I wouldn't care if you said you'll hold your breath till you face turns blue.

I know you are thinking; how could he be so cold.

It's just a reaction to all the lies I was told.

Change Time
By: R.J. Edwards

I shouldn't have walked out of your life

I was stupid I should have made you my wife

It's my fault that you've been through all that you've been through

Only if I would have known the things that you would
endure because I chose to delete our score

I would change my mind because I never would
want you to endure those things

I'm so sorry our love wasn't clear to me

I believe both our lives would be so different

We would both still be successful

But our lives wouldn't be so stressful

Let's be the reason each other smile and go that extra mile

To help erase those bad memories and erase
those thoughts of those now enemies.

Why
By: R.J. Edwards

Why is it that you let us suffer first?

For you were the one who let us be born to a mother who didn't love us.

It's crazy as you knew she was lazy and getting paid from child support

While giving no support and you wonder why I'm a poor sport.

No one was there to cheer for me and show me the ropes.

Both of my parents were alive but were dead to me.

Was this for you to build a fighting spirit within.

All it really did was make me hold my emotions
within and even as a youngster,

I dibbled with gin as I knew already how to
sin due to the lack of guidance,

They just lucky they never heard those sirens.

Why did you pick those parents for me?

They were both busy running them streets not
even making sure I had something to eat.

If it wasn't for my sister, I wouldn't even be sure I'd be here today.

As she always looked to make a way,

But it was a pretty price she had to pay, I thank her to this day.

I leave you with this question why should I pray
to you when you let us die every day?

Deception
By: R.J. Edwards

When you fed my ego, I didn't want to let you go.

That was my worst mistake,

For that was your plan this whole time.

To gain my trust and do anything you must to get it

Like sending me naked pictures.

Showing up to my door step in nothing but a trench

Telling me how much you liked my deep stroke

How I didn't see those lies,

Right, you did a wonderful job pulling the wool over my eyes.

I just want to know how you live with yourself.

Knowing that you only have what you have because of someone else.

Missed Opportunity
By: R.J. Edwards

Due to my issues I lost you

I know due to your job you were afraid to commit too

I should have shown you I was in it to win it

I was young and inexperienced

In loving a woman who had her head on her shoulders

Wish I could crave someone like you by chipping away at a boulder

That can't happen

Now all I can do is thinking about what we could have been

Maybe like four kids

A nice big crib

Married for a couple years

Knowing you we would have boohoo a million tears

Man, those would have been some great years

Too bad we couldn't get away from our fears

What
By: R.J. Edwards

What did I do to deserve punishment for the next man's sins?

Like we were Siamese twins, or he was my next to kin.

All I did was admire you,

I was on my way to making all your dreams come true.

Feeling this hidden hate, you have for me leaves me so
clueless and have me feel like such a buffoon.

It got me wishing I was a cartoon,

Wishing I could just erase my past,

For this hurt wouldn't last.

Did you do it because you thought the grass was greener?

Was it just part of you plan to make sure your future was brighter?

Either way I hope you meet someone who is a whole lot meaner.

That way you'll know what it feels like to be misled by a deceiver.

Bad Decisions
By: R.J. Edwards

Can you imagine if you had the power to stop yourself from
making all the bad decisions you've made in this life

I don't know about you

But my pockets would be fatter

Wouldn't have no baby mamas

Everything probably would be mine

Like yeah that's my motorcycle

Yeah that's my Bentley coupe

Oh, that old thing yeah that's just my old school I pull out on the weekend

I wish I could go back in time and hit myself with a couple of one liners

Like don't feel bad it was just that

A one nightstand you're not supposed to be her man

Or you broke up with her you ain't got to be
nice and celebrate her birthday

Lastly but not least

Yes, she's a freak but does she really have your back in these streets

Man, oh man if I would have just listened to
that voice in the back of my brain

I wouldn't be sitting here wishing someone could take away this pain

Pain
By: R.J. Edwards

Pain!

What can you really gain from it?

Besides knowing that you are hurt.

And need comfort.

Can it really be motivation?

Like seeing your mom get beat,

Being left in the street with nothing to eat,

Like seeing your sister get beat,

I know it sounds like a repeat.

But you should have seen the fear in their eyes.

There was nothing he could do but be a witness to the brutality.

He would just hide in his room to try and dismiss the sounds.

But his father didn't know that that is what got him aroused.

He put a plan together for that one day he could be
there for his mother and again for his sister.

So, pain can be a motivator if you pay attention
to the signs and get off your behind.

Or next thing you know you'll be next on
that ass whooping assembly line!

Lost ones Pt. 1
By: R.J. Edwards

You were so beautiful the first day I laid eyes on
you and got to be in your presence.

It would be a long time before we really get to know each

Years went by, but I could always see the beautiful spirit in your eyes

Even after I saw your failed relationships.

I still steered my ship into your path.

Knowing one day I'll be the one to make the connection between us last.

For I loved you so much I waited to the right
moment to give you the gentlest touch.

The first kiss for me was a start of a new journey.

As I never wanted to leave your side but as our
journey got started, I had to say goodbye

It wasn't because our bond wasn't connected

It was to finish a dream I started the first time I met you

To make more money than any one in our family has
ever seen and live a life like you and I dreamed.

Due to that journey our light went dimmer with every year
that passed by for you found yourself another guy

It broke my heart for from the start

Since I told you I was coming back to you from
the dark place where we found our spark

I guess you felt like it was going to be a broken promise
as we both knew what words meant coming from love
ones that didn't do what they really meant

All I could do was finish the dream which I did but
why oh why did it have to cost me My Queen.

Just an Ex
By: R.J. Edwards

I can't even text now.

That got me like wow!

Whenever you were around me you never wore a frown.

Cos you know I'm a straight up clown.

You know how we use to get down.

But I get it

It's not cool

Cause I'm just an ex now

I can't even tag you in funny pictures no more.

For the fear of you might block me

It wasn't like that when I had you under lock and key

Well I guess it's kind of weird now

As I'm just an ex now.

It's so funny that you act this way now.

Cos every time you see me you can't fight that pretty smile

I know our time together is far behind like we've run a mile

I truly can't believe you just treat me like I'm an ex now.

Just know every time I look at you all I can say is wow!

That's a special gal.

Mischievous
By: R.J. Edwards

I told you my secrets and you turned around and used them against me

All the things I did for you and you chose to be so disloyal

Now we don't mix like water and oil

What happened to building towards what you wished for?

Come to find out you just plotted so you could get more

Damn only if I could have seen into the future what you had in store

Turns out you were just a big money hungry whore.

It's cool though for out of the drama and strife I was lucky you
never became my wife which would have cost me galore.

Just know to me you'll always be dead like you got six to the head.

Understand
By: R.J. Edwards

I don't understand why you would do this to our plans.

When you said yes when I put that ring on your hand.

All the memories we've made are now gone.

Now I only get to see them in a distance as I would be reminiscing.

For I use to see them every time I saw you smiling.

How I made you happy,

That gave me a reason to be proud

As I know what you've been through.

A good man in your life is what I wanted to prove to you that I was

Not someone here to cause you more damage
and leave you stranded and abandoned.

But to show you that you are a flower just in need of some good loving

I did all these things for years.

Yet you choose to leave me in tears.

I just don't understand why you would do such a thing.

But I forgot fear has been ruining love for years.

Why
By: R.J. Edwards

Why do you feel I'm that guy?

Is it because you feel I'm easy on the eye?

What is it about me that makes you feel I'm the one?

I could be as dumb as a drum,

Or even worst drinking rum till my body goes numb.

But do you know why I would do that?

I don't think you would because you don't know me.

For it could be because I was abused as a young man.

Told how dumb I would be since I was three.

Or how about because I had to sell drugs to get myself through school.

How I had to provide for myself before I could vote.

You wonder why I act the way I do.

It was because my childhood was voided.

For I had to become a man before my time because the
one who made me was nowhere to be found.

Why would you want to be with me as my life
has produce a man that can go cold?

For the love I was supposed to be given was always on hold.

Are you the one to take it off hold for me?

So, I can be bold and explore the world of love and so much more.

Like raising a family that never sees the other side of the score.

Show me why love should be a part of me for I need more.

To live for more than providing for loved ones that set out for a score.

Please show me why love is the number one thing people try to avoid.

I want to be helplessly in love with my family I thought I'd never score

Why the long pause did I scare you?

Are you just thinking how I could care for you through this pain?

And live my life against the grain?

Just know I know why I am here

I just wonder why you'd want to do the same

FANTASY

Dream
By: R.J. Edwards

Who would have thought in a million years I
would run into someone like you?

So beautiful intelligent smart and sexy, even in blue.

Who loves me for me times three with my rules.

I'm here truly to give you the key to my heart.

For I never want us anymore to be apart.

As you are my dream woman.

From your head to your toes especially when you are fully clothed.

You are so far from something I've ever dreamed,
you are truly so special to me.

No one can stand next to you without feeling your greatness that is within.

When we're separated I feel so restless.

For I know My Queen is gone and I feel so helpless.

But, I know it's not for long.

For I wasn't stupid I made sure I got you down that aisle

Now, we have two things that match.

Our last names and our smiles.

Trust I plan to keep both there till we're both in the ground.

For you are my dream woman and I always plan to
service you with a smile all year around.

I Wish
By: R.J. Edwards

I wish: I could change the past

I wish: I could see the future

I wish: we could have been closer

I wish: I could take away all the pain

I wish: you could have shown me you loved me

I wish: I could have accomplished more

I wish: I could fix all that you wished

I wish: I could do so much more

But even if I could

Would that bring you to my door?

For you was an absentee father who could have done so much more

I thought making it to the pros would give us a chance
but all I received from you was an open hand

How could you when you weren't even a man?

So, here I wish that through it all I could shake the hand
of the man who refused to get know his son at all

For I can show you that I'm nothing like you at all

My plan is to make men out of my sons and
support them through life and have a ball

For I know that in that I'm really nothing like you at all.

Missing
By: R.J. Edwards

I wish we could just hop in the shower.

So, we could stay in there for about an hour.

Get drunk on each other.

Melting each other's hands like butter.

But, you are nowhere to be found.

That's why I always wear a frown.

Can I Get?
By: R.J. Edwards

Can I get:

A Woman who is not just out for my cash

Think I'm supposed to spend on her just because she got a lot of ass

Also, on that same note, how is it that this is all she's got to bring to the table is some good sex no wonder she got a phonebook worth of ex's

As she always scheming for some checks

Not knowing she's only leaving others' lives in a wreck

Causing them to never want to love again

Which I think is one of the biggest sins

For love can heal all and help you live life like there's no tomorrow

You just living on time that's burrowed

Can I get:

To see our men and women get along to build
a family and not just make a child

For more than likely the man is going to disappear and not be there to guide the child leaving it with more chances of running wild

Make sure you always go that extra mile to make each other smile

As that will insure that you two will stay around for a while and most importantly guide that child into a brighter future for tomorrow

Not leave them in bed with a heart full of sorrow

Can I get:

A Queen that knows she's a Queen

Do you know what I mean?

One that never tilts her head knowing that her crown might fall

One that knows her confidence will make her stand out from all the rest

One that knows that the emblem placed on her chest is a
constant reminder that that she is truly one of the best

For all those who are Queens

Please

You must put the wicked games to rest

So

We can walk in our greatness together today and a lifetime of tomorrows.

A Woman
By: R.J. Edwards

I would love to have

A woman

That will help me activate my left and right brain

A woman

That will help me heal this pain

A woman

That knows my love knows no shame

A woman

That's willing to change her last name

A woman

That knows our love is no game

A woman

That is not just here for the fame

A woman

Who knows my aims

A woman

Who knows I'd never be ashamed to claim

A woman

Who knows how to keep be a spark to the flames

A woman

Who's not looking to be put in a frame

A woman

Who's not afraid to play life's big bad game

I
By: R.J. Edwards

I

Dare you

Not to fear the unknown

I

Dare you

To embrace all failures

I

Dare you

To overcome all obstacles

I

Dare you

Never to allow yourself to be down

I

Dare you

To realize you are a conqueror

What If
By: R.J. Edwards

What if we did it?

Held each other in an embrace

Would it be warm and comforting or would it be cold and disastrous?

What if we did it?

Held each other's hand with our fingers intertwined

Would it be electric and send tingles down our spine
or make us realize we've lost our minds?

What if we did it?

Kissed and allowed our tongues to do a happy dance.

Would it be the start of a new beginning or would
it be better if we were just dreaming?

What if we never did any of it and just remained best of friends?

Would we always wonder what could have been?

Would we be performing a disastrous sin?

By not looking for happiness within each other and making what
we have so much deeper than being each other keepers of secrets

Guess we'll never know but our friendship will also flow

For we never crossed any of those forbidden bridges
and climbed into each other britches.

If and Will
By: R.J. Edwards

If I read to you,

Will you adore me?

If I cook for you,

Will you admire me?

If I bring you flowers every day,

Will you love me?

These are the many questions that run through
my mind as time passes by.

Wondering what it would take for you to be mine.

How could I cherish my Queen without giving her a ring?

Is it just by doing the trivial things?

I feel if I turn my ifs into I do,

You should never be wondering or questioning if I love you.

Airport Thought
By: R.J. Edwards

I'm sitting in the airport waiting on this cutie pie.

My oh my,

How fine she is.

Butter pecan skin,

Beautiful ass,

Tasty lips oh and don't forget about the hips

With a brain to match.

The total package enough to give you a heart attack.

But why oh why does she always look so mean

Is it because she's a fiend?

No, not for drugs but for someone to love and to
cherish and walk down the aisle for marriage

As she looked at me in my eye,

I know she's wondering can I be that guy...

Crown
By: R.J. Edwards

You want people to stay around with you always wearing a frown.

Come on you suppose to be happy you were born to wear a crown.

Why is it that you're always down?

Do you need a trip out of town?

I know what it is, you are still dealing with that clown!

What do I have to show you for you to know I'm
the one who's supposed to be around?

Crazy
By: R.J. Edwards

You said you would be there for me no matter what and now you're gone.

That's crazy!

You said you had plans for our future and
now you're nowhere to be found.

That's crazy!

You said you wanted to marry me, have kids with
me and make our branch of the family tree

And now I see no resemblance of thee.

That's crazy!

You said so many things to me and it made me so happy.

Only to turn around to find out it was more than two fists full of lies.

Which is crazy for it was my bed in which your
head would lay on any given day.

All because I knew you were gonna make me a happy lady.

But that day never came.

And I felt so ashamed.

For falling yet again,

For the sweet words of another lame.

A boy proclaiming to be a man,

Yet only thing that makes you that is what it is that you hold in your hand.

Which is crazy for I was there to stand by your side and be your Queen,

And everything in between.

But you rather chase after loose skirts just because
they like you without your shirt.

Not knowing you just lost your Queen.

Which is going to be a hard pill to swallow,

And leave you feeling hollow.

But, that is life as crazy as it seems.

Guy
By: R.J. Edwards

I don't do all the things I do for you to try
and convince you I'm a nice guy.

No, I'm that guy who will give you everything
thing you are looking for and more

I'll run to the store

Give you flowers on random days

Run you bath water when you say you're sore.

How about rubbing your feet as a treat because you're so sweet?

Yes, I'm that guy who plays for keeps,

If you leave me, it wasn't because my love was weak or
because I was out here running in these streets

It will have to be because you felt I was too good for you.

Because you couldn't love and appreciate me like you were supposed to.

You let the guys before me cloud your judgment

Not knowing what I was up to

I just wanted to be that guy who spoiled you

After you got out the shower rub oil on you

When it's cold outside, cuddle you

Most importantly I wanted to be your man for
if all else fails you know I got you.

Son
By R.J Edwards

No matter what I've down throughout my day, I'm
never too tired to give you some play.

It's my joy to put a smile on your face each day

Through the sunshine, through the rain,

And through the snow.

There's nothing that will stop me from getting to you,

For you are my source of life.

My main goal is to be everything to you that I have never had.

So, know my son if I'm hard on you it's not to make you sad or mad.

It's to make sure you never do what I did because I didn't have a Dad.

I Meant It
By: R.J. Edwards

I don't try to win you over with words I put together about you.

I do it to show you, I admire the person that I see.

If it was up to me it would be three or more of us in a store.

For you would be my family and we'd be watching
our kid run through the open door.

See you would be my wife bearing my last name.

And putting all those rumors to shame,

That I couldn't just be with one dame.

But me and you we never worry about the thoughts
of others long as we had each other

Now with our heir here ready to carry on the legacy.

I know I prove to you that all the things I said about you were true.

And not just a way to get to you.

For I made you a wife than a mother.

For after I saw you I knew there would be no other.

FAR AWAY

Journey
By: R.J. Edwards

I'm glad I could be your one in a billion.

The who's allowed admission into your theme park.

I knew one day I would get my golden ticket to your chocolate factory.

Now are you going to hand over the keys, so I can take over?

Being the one that will show you so much more
than you ever thought you would explore,

I'm the one you've always been looking for and I
followed the rules to get close to you.

Even though we crossed paths and I didn't score,

Now we are here again, and I'm going to score
and show you so much more.

I was the one from before and I owe you from before.

I knew you captured my eye,

But I was a young man whose plan was to live life as high as the sky.

Only then did I realize you was that ribbon in the sky I was chasing

For we were so far apart wishing.

I had to elevate to escape the temptation and
pitfalls to live out my fate with you

Only then could I see our love would be true.

Now I can't see a me without you!

Disappear
By: R.J. Edwards

Why are you here?

Why don't you just disappear?

Is it fear that is keeping you here?

Don't you know that me hurting you is coming near?

You need to get away from hear.

As I have no fear in leaving you standing here with a handful of tears.

Truly, why are you here?

Why don't you just disappear?

Love is not near,

Is that not clear?

You're just standing around waiting to shed another tear.

Again, why are you here?

Why don't you just disappear?

Has love faded so much that you're willing
to wait around for it to reappear?

Never chase something you've lost, as it's already a faded memory.

For the last time, why are you here?

Why don't you just disappear?

Proud and Loud
By: R.J. Edwards

Why weren't you in the stands screaming loudly?

How come I didn't have you standing there proudly?

I never did it for the cheer of the fans.

I did it for one day I will hear you say, "That's my little man."

I wanted to hear you scream my name,

But, all I ended up getting was a little fame.

I got all I could handle from that fame except some little shame.

Even the star was of a couple of those games.

Never did I hear those words that I wanted to hear,

Because you never showed up and that was really a shame.

But, I still wonder why you weren't in the stands screaming loudly!

Or, how come I didn't have you standing there proudly!

Future
By: R.J. Edwards

Let's take a walk on the beach and hold hands.

Let's talk about our grand plans.

Let's escape to a faraway land.

Let's make sure we always take a stand.

For we'll never know when this could all end.

Where
By: R.J. Edwards

Where were you when I needed you the most?

There was so much pain and agony of not having you there.

To hold my hand,

To make the plan,

To take a stand,

To count my first million,

To give me your crazy opinion,

To teach me how to fix an engine,

And to let me know I'd be okay after I tore my tendon.

Where were you when I needed you the most?

ALONE

Alone
By: R.J. Edwards

When I was born,

Who knew I would be alone?

I wish I had a clone.

Someone who knew me and wanted to be with me.

Not someone who at every moment looked to disown me.

What did I do to deserve this?

Is this something I earned from a past life?

If it is, I must have been living real strife.

To be misled, used and abused,

I must have really been one bad dude.

I guess I didn't deserve a second chance,

To make a stance,

To improve and be good.

I guess that's why I never made it out of the hood.

Dream
By: R.J. Edwards

The dream is fading into the darkness.

Who would've thought I couldn't handle this loneliness.

Should I settle for the American's dream of a wife and a family.

Why?

I do have no apathy towards that type of life.

Sorry, you can leave me without a bride.

Now, I will just go on enjoying this lonely ride.

Think
By: R.J. Edwards

Think! Why should I?

All I do is seem to make is mistakes.

I guess I just don't have what it takes.

To love or be loved.

How do I solve it?

Why does it have to be solved?

Can't I live a life being myself?

I'm tired of the let downs.

Been through so much and I stay looking like a clown.

No more because there's a new sheriff in town.

The king is shining up his new crown.

You'll never see this King wearing a frown

As I am the source of my happiness.

I'm through dealing with women and their craftiness

It's time to just focus on that person which is me.

For that will be the key.

Mystery
By: R.J. Edwards

You wonder why you always see me alone.

A King never wants to share his throne.

I would let you get close to me,

But for fear of you hurting me.

You'll never truly be close to me as if we were
standing together but in between us is a tree.

You say that's sad for you'll never find true love.

I'd say it's okay cause eagles soar alone, and I
never want to consider myself a dove.

I'm always willing to show love.

Just know I will be doing so from up above,

Until I find one that soars like me,

I will be sticking to this sad little story.

Absent
By: R.J. Edwards

When I slipped,

Why weren't you there to catch me?

Am I a disappointment in your eyes?

Was it because you told me not to hang with those guys?

What is it?

For you are the reason that I am here.

But, I have never known what it feels like to have you near.

ALONE
By: R.J. Edwards

I was born into this city alone,

Nobody was Home.

My pops abandon me at birth,

Mom took interest in whatever guy that was paying
attention to what was up her skirt.

I ended roaming the cold streets and made the city my home

I was grown at a youthful age

I never really took to authority

For rules really bored me

As I was the one who made sure I was fresh
to death and didn't starve to death

Why was it I had to answer to you?

I came to realize to make it you had to know how to shake and bake

I mean you had to know how to make the right moves as lions and
lioness was waiting in the grass to take full advantage of you

Mislead your unguarded and naive ass

They didn't get me in those hard days as I always looked to cover my ass

I kept the grass cut to see every last one of their slithering ass

It wasn't till I got comfortable and pockets full of
dough that I started to let the weeds show

Thinking I could change them into something more as I've came from
the bottom and made it to the top due to a couple helping hands

Little did I know they were chameleons waiting to take a
true stand against me and everything I've worked for and
to somehow do more damage to me than ever before

So, stay on your toes at the bottom and the top as
it's always people lurking to make you drop

It's cool to be alone as even a star shines bright
by itself if not for no one else

But, if you venture off for a team make sure
you truly share the same dream.

WOMEN

Women
By: R.J. Edwards

How beautiful you are!

So graceful but also so bizarre.

Why is it that I can only choose one of you out of nine?

When I can make you all happy and smile,

And also still go that extra mile.

Buying gifts and giving you quality time.

I just want all of you to be mine.

I know I can't have this.

But I want it all the time.

Damn, why do women have to be so damn fine?

I know it does not seem right,

But is it so wrong,

To want to have just as many women that DMX named in his song?

I know it takes a wedding ring for you to be mine.

But, I can't do it because you all are just too damn fine.

Woman
By: R.J. Edwards

Why are you looking so mean?

For through you, every girl becomes a Queen.

Your life is precious for you have the power to give it.

Know that without you there is no reason for me to exist.

Don't be so dismissive when a King approaches cause if you
watched his moves, he's only looking to bless you not test you.

You are the power to his legacy as all would die with him without you.

You are amazing and beautiful if only the world
knew what to truly do with you.

Love and nurturing comes so easy for you I
guess that's why you're so powerful.

You are a Queen stop living your life as if it doesn't have meaning.

Miss Independent
By: R.J. Edwards

She's so beautiful, gorgeous and stunning.

That woman got her own money,

car and a house.

The only reason I'll get a chance is because she's without a spouse.

I wonder is it because of the venom she spits out of her mouth.

She's an independent woman who can live without a man up in her house

Trying to lock her down with all his rules.

I'm just going to introduce myself to that sweet lady
and tell her I ain't about nothing shady.

I don't want to be doing all this talking

I'm going to show you through my attention to
detail why you should be my lady

For we can build an empire together and if we don't like
where we are at, we can always change the weather

That means take trips.

On ships or place we go skinny dip

My plan for us is to make the world our toys.

So, are you with that or are you thinking this is just a trap?

For this just sounds like a smooth rap

Trust me I wouldn't waste your time or mine.

As life is a battlefield and you never know when it's your time.

INSPIRATIONS

Pill
By: R.J. Edwards

Taking pills is not an excuse

To help you get loose as a goose.

It's an escape drug.

That will end up being a plug.

To all your hopes and dreams,

Leaving you on the corner begging for a dollar and cream.

What does this mean?

Get out of your own way.

Today can be the day;

You change up your games.

You stop hanging with those no names.

Have a plan to be a better man,

Owning houses and land.

Be someone people can look up to.

Not just someone they knew.

Give the kids your version of being successful,

Not showing them how life can be so stressful.

Growth is key in this world.

Now get up out of the dirty murk and leave that junk behind.

Show the next generation how to really work and grind.

Let Me
By: R.J. Edwards

Let me teach you from my mistake

Forever thing you come across ain't always great

Most are here just to take up space

Most of your homeboys who you think are your ace

Are just in line like everybody else trying to see
what you are going to put on their plate

Don't you hate when people got the same twenty-four hours as you

And you see them relaxing around like they ain't got anything to do

But soon as the first of the month come around
the first person they are calling is you

Then you got to hit them with the nah fam, I ain't even got it

Knowing that you do they keep asking like a bum for a dollar

You almost break then you remember they were
nowhere around before you got this far

They stayed at the bar tossing them back

While you were in the gym with about eight hundred pounds on you back

Remember the struggle and how far you've came

For to lose it all because you're helping those
who didn't help you would be a shame.

Relationships
By: R.J. Edwards

Life is an adventure

Full of twists and turns

To outlast it all your love must really burn for the other

Like how someone loves their grandmother

I mean it must be hot enough to melt precious metals

That way through it all it'll be as you're walking on rose petals.

Be an Example
By: R.J. Edwards

Skies are blue

My shades are red

Before I leave this earth, my kids will know the
difference between good and bad.

I will be a dad there to guide them and not be absent

Show them what it means to carry the worries
of your family on your back like

When a man loved a woman and a woman loved her man

And they willingly walked through the trenches together hand and hand

Willing to face public death if their love was banned.

Be the like our forefather, who would do all they could to
make sure that their love for their family was understood.

Facts
By: R.J. Edwards

The biggest lie you can tell yourself is telling
yourself that it's not that simple

Man

Life is just like popping a pimple

Things are going to come up

Either you going to pop it or try and cover it

But either one that you do

Some bullshit is still going to find you

Always be ready for the bullshit as it might be you that it's next to test

Handling the crazy obstacles in this world especially in your quest for love

As everyone is out here playing for keeps in these so called mean streets

Guarding the ring like Sméagol

Not knowing that if you team up with the right intent to
create greatness you would both will soar like eagles

But we are stuck in the mindset that what's mine is mine and
you don't deserve a dime, or my time is usually the line

Not knowing that thinking is so out of line

As they want you thinking you can do it all by yourself

Remember it's easy to break one stick

So, truly think about it

Ain't it easier to get jumped when you're all alone

Do what's right and turn your house into a home.

Uncertainty
By: R.J. Edwards

The life I lead is full of thorns.

At one point I thought I was lying in a bed full of roses.

Sleeping with wolves that were in sheep clothing.

Lessons can be learned every step of the way,

Just make sure that you're able to come out okay.

Pain is there because growth is needed,

Just ask the kid who touched the stove when he didn't think it was heated.

Spend your life on the dream you want to see come to reality

Not doing things because of a technicality.

Searching for love and settling for the wrong guy
because you're tired of being lonely.

Settling for anything that is not your dream is living a life as a phony.

You only have one life to live solely.

There is going to be plenty of mistakes.

Please don't settle for anything less than great.

For when you are on your death bed it's going to be hard to forgive.

Dream
By: R.J. Edwards

There is no cost for you to dream.

As it's free to dream like a free-flowing stream.

Realize there's no cost for you to dream.

Think about all the things you can redeem.

If you have courage enough to dream,

Go boldly after it till you make everyone scream.

For you chase you dream and achieved.

Dreams will come to you daily.

Don't allow fear to make you lazy.

Before you know it, you'll be pushing up daisy.

All your dreams are dying and they came to
you, so you could give them to life

Instead you choose to dim the lights.

Compassion
By: R.J. Edwards

What is compassion to you?

Is it only what others can do for you?

Compassion should have love built in every single action you make.

From baking a cake,

To admitting you made a mistake.

Compassion brings about forgiveness,

Not causing more sadness.

It allows you to let go of the unimportant things.

While building to better things.

A solid foundation has compassion in the mixture.

It will bring about a better future.

Don't be a hard-hearted person due to all the wrongs done to you.

Allow you compassion to flow through you and just
watch how the world will open to you.

I Remember
By: R.J. Edwards

I remember writing papers under the hallway lights late at night.

I remember not being able to watch nick at night.

I remember getting touched on and thinking this ain't right.

I remember having to get home before the street lights.

I remember signing those college papers and
thinking I'm going to make things right

I remember all those street fights.

I remember my dad never tucking me in at night.

I remember feeling like this can't be life.

I remember the day I knew I made it.

I remember the day I knew my gear would never be outdated

I remember how I use to get faded.

I remember how they told me I'll never make it

I remember everything from the good to the bad

Yes, it was many days I thought I wouldn't last

I knew these tough times would come to pass,

And the man they were making was going to be ahead of any class.

I Remember Pt. 2
By: R.J. Edwards

I remember being denied a mother's love.

I remember praying to the God above,

Wondering why I don't know what it's like to be loved.

I remember being over looked.

I remember when I knew I had what it took.

I remember being doubted from the outlook.

I remember family telling me I would never be as good my cousin.

I remember realizing that wasn't going to be my reality.

I remember working hard to be a standout.

I remember the day I worked for what came about.

I remember when Love was my drug for I never knew what it was about.

I remember thinking how the people who were supposed
to love me try to fill me with so much doubt.

I remember telling myself I must work harder than ever
so I would never have to live check to check.

I remember signing a deal knowing I would I
always have enough money on deck.

I Thought
By: R.J. Edwards

I just knew my life was heading in the right direction.

I thought there was an option.

I just had a healthy baby boy and signed a new deal.

You would have thought,

My life was heading towards endless happy adventures and thoughts.

So, I thought.

Turns out it was the beginning of many downfalls

So, I thought

Those so-called downfalls were blessings in disguise.

Allowed me to see who my devoted friends were.

Let me know I really wasn't in love with her.

Now those years to me is just a blur.

So, I thought.

As I still must live with those wild decisions.

Not to mention.

Leaving a game, I loved without maxing out my pension.

Lesson learned.

Don't allow distractions to uproot you from your main attraction.

Special
By: R.J. Edwards

When I look out all I see is blue

Mermaids singing to me, come down here it's more things for you to do

I drive deeper into the forbidden glories

Only to be washed up on shore with plenty of horror stories

Don't allow yourself to be overwhelmed with the wonders of this orld

Doing things that would make most people want to hurl

For you are so unique that there is only one of you

Remember this always for people won't be able to
discourage you of the things you really want to do.

Forty-Five
By: R.J. Edwards

They say you shouldn't argue with a fool because from
a distance people don't know who is who

It's fucked up our country men and women voted for one

Just to think his run has just begun

When will we ever learn not to pick someone who don't
understand what it's like to live without none

We know now that our next couple of years is going to under the gun

Of a tyrant who believes he is the answer to all our problems

Not knowing he's only making things worse as he acts worst than toddlers

I wonder if people know what they know now about his actions

Would they still support him?

Or would they try and deport him if they could?

As they all know now he's truly no good.

Growth
By: R.J. Edwards

I am the author of my own story

Some of the characters didn't belong but made a feature

Due to the creature I had become in that moment in my life

I had lost a wife due to divorce

What's worse?

I lost half my net worth.

No wonder I was looking for a stress reliever

But messed around and turned that stress into a bigger cleaver

Luckily for me I was still living the dream

Receiving more cream than I've ever dreamed

Only to let the one thing I desired the most cause me so
much pain and made me not able to maintain

My focus

Not able to see you everyday

Made everything be in disarray

Just know I'm working always to make sure we're going to be okay

Never letting stress see another part of our day no
matter what danger may come our way

Self-Talk
By: R.J. Edwards

Man

You got stop doing that shit

You know your girl is it

The one you want to spend the rest of your life with

So, why are you out here creeping with this other bitch?

You keep this up

You'll be looking for another chick

Don't act like you don't give a shit

You know you'd be sick.

For you haven't ever met another who was so about you

Take care of you

Love you

Understood you

Stood by you

Probably would die for you

So, why do you want to be a fool and keep putting her
through what you are putting her through?

It's really time for you to get a clue

Before she's leaves you without a clue of what to do.

Deep
By: R.J. Edwards

Come here and let me undress your insecurities

Relax as I fuck away your fears

You've been waiting for this for years

Allowing you to shed tears of joy as you now know
now you can say bye to those fuck boys

Let's take a shower to wash away those filthy things
and we can watch them go down the drain

For they can never come back and run a train on your emotions

Let's dress you in the garments of the Queen that you are

Like happiness, joy, love, compassion, loyalty, and truthfulness

I don't believe there is anything we missed

Oops your crown of integrity

Never again letting the trivial things bother you
on your path to your true destiny

Education
By: R.J. Edwards

Don't let the world educate you or your child

Be proud to pick up and read multiple books

For if you depend on what you'd be taught in this world you'd be lost.

More than half the stuff they teach is false

Don't fall victim to the trap of all you need is a school education

For they are the same ones who wrote the emancipation proclamation

Giving us false hope of a better life

Then also turned around and found multiple ways to kill us left and right

Still till this day they still ain't treating us right

Educate yourself and your child for the good fight

For the days ahead can be better than just alright.

True or False
By: R.J. Edwards

Life is life

Bills are bills

Thrills are thrills

The thing that is priceless is when someone is real.

I Need All Three
By: R.J. Edwards

I want you to like it

As that gets your attention

I need you to love it

As that means you will always want it

I need you to lust for it

As it says you will do anything for it

Doubt
R.J. Edwards

It's crazy how people give you reasons why you should doubt.

Why you should take a different route.

Dreams and goals won't be filled easy

If you have integrity and don't want to do anything greasy.

Please believe me there are alternative routes.

But, you should never have a reason to doubt.

Just get on your grind and show them what you got.

Then they'll know they were foolish to doubt.

When you've finished, make sure you stand tall.

All they wanted to see was you to fall.

Be humble in your victory.

As this is not the end of your story.

She or He, Don't force it
By: R.J. Edwards

If _____ is not easy like a summer breeze

Don't force it

If _____ is like peddling a bike with no gears up hill

Don't force it

If _____ don't have you day dreaming
about the times you were together

Don't force it

If _____ don't make you smile when _____ is not even around

Don't force it

If _____don't have you feeling like a firework when you kiss

Don't force it

If _____ don't get you wet or hard thinking about it

Don't force it

If _____ don't make you think about future plans

Don't force it

If _____ don't make you want to start a new life

Don't force it

Love can make you do some crazy things

Like picking out rings with so much bling

Just to see him or her smile for a while before the next thing

As the poem says don't force it if he or she can't have you
thinking life without him or her is just a thing

Better
By: R.J. Edwards

With everything in you, you tried to break me

But here I stand a grown ass man

Life so much better since we don't walk hand in hand anymore

Good thing too as life has showed me there is so much more in store

Brand new place

In a new space

Don't have the Devil smiling in my face

Would you look at how I've been shown crazy grace

Life is full of many ups and downs

I be damned if I walk around wearing a frown

Instead it will be a massive crown

For I am a King and I will sing it loud and proud

For when I'm in a crowd my energy will be contagious, and
they will see how I've vowed never to let life get me down

Live Your Life
By: R.J. Edwards

If I would have listened to everyone else's opinion about what I couldn't do

I would

Still be in the hood up to no good

Chasing tail, in and out of jail

Just another failure and once again the system would have prevailed.

Selling dope to all my kin folk thinking it's really the way to live

Old people on the porch thinking what gives

Not knowing I'm part of the reason Martin Luther King's Dream is dying

If I said this how I thought my life would be going I'd be lying.

Most importantly I would have let my life be
consumed be other people's fears

That's why I'm glad I chose to face my fears.

As I now have a fist full of tears.

From all those struggling years.

I reach my goal, through determination and sacrifice,

I'm glad I didn't allow those nay-sayers to
convince me to put my dreams on ice.

My Life Pt. 1
By: R.J. Edwards

I don't know why I do the shit that I do.

Probably because I was misled more than you.

Think about it

mama wasn't around

I had a deadbeat dad

Doesn't this story already sound sad?

I was abused in more ways than one.

Even though it gives me something to brag about like it was fun.

I'm older now and they should be ashamed of the shit they've done.

I was stripped of my innocence and by the way did I tell you about how I had a gun pointed dead in my face and wasn't scared to run.

I just wished he'd pulled the trigger

If he did guess what I would have just been another dead nigger.

My Life Pt. 2
By: R.J. Edwards

The story goes on as all that happened before the age of twelve

I know I was a young child living in hell

Guess what sports broke that spell.

It gave me a way out of that so-called jail

Sports put me around people who believe in foresight

Which gave me the might to change my life and work on doing almost everything right

Got to say I had no real support system at home and tell you the truth in high school I was damn near grown.

Able to roam the streets even after the lights came on

All I had to do was make it home before the alarm was put on

I never lost sight of being more of a father than my sperm donor was.

I would push myself to exhaustion because I knew
no one else was willing to do what I was.

It all paid off too for I had our phone ringing with crazy buzz.

I became a top recruit in football and was heading
to a big college to play some ball

Know you can write your own story

Even though those closest to you truly want to see you fall.

Don't Do It
By: R.J. Edwards

Don't you know no woman you meet is going to be a nun?

You shouldn't worry about getting none

For you are a superstar in the making.

Every time you have sex it's like she has a gun

Ready to rob you for all the work hard you've done

Is she really a reason to get hard for?

I'm place in your life to help you not make the choices I made

Some nights I wish I stayed home and played some spades

Me being me I was horny and was looking to get laid

Don't get me wrong I love you more than life itself

It's just your mother is something else

The Gag
By: R.J. Edwards

I got more layers to me than your favorite cake

Shared some with the wrong people and that was my mistake

It's crazy how your own people don't want to see you be great.

They want to be the reason for your downfall

I'm just going to use it as motivation and show
them how you truly raise above it all

Like endless trips to the mall

How life is supposed to be a straight ball

Leaving them wishing for another chance at it all

Wake Up
By: R.J. Edwards

If slavery was a choice,

Then why is it the black men is getting hung till this day?

You must not have heard about that in your mansion.

Black people get eat up out here like we live next door to Charles Manson.

I must say, with what you are saying we won't
even think about paying your ransom.

Better
By: R.J. Edwards

Sometimes you're a bad judge of character.

For you got a big heart.

It's okay because not everyone is blessed with that type of art.

Just know next time you must be smart.

Not everybody deserves to be able to be in your cart.

Strive for Greatness
By: R.J. Edwards

Work till you don't have a bad angle

They can't shoot you from anywhere and
they'll always catch your good side

Beside it not all about the glitz and the glamour

It's about being here to your last hour.

You have dreams to reach

Children to teach

Live to give that great speech

That does not only seal your legacy.

Will teach those behind you and that look up to
you that their dreams are not out of reach

You're going to have to put in long hours

Be looked at like a Debbie downer

Work when you could be out partying

It's a small price to pay for your guardian

Just know a legacy don't come to those who don't grind.

It comes to those who's willing to be last in the present.

For in the future

They will truly show you how to shine

For money is the last thing that they must worry about at any time.

Outside Looking In
By: R.J. Edwards

I look at you my sister as a Queen.

All you want to do to is show everyone that you are not nice

And if you weren't human your heart would probably be made from ice

Your attitude is as careless as a driver in an action scene.

But you still want guys to spoil you and adore you.

Don't you know you are never going to find him?

That would be like mixing water with oil

I know I don't mean to be rude.

But someone must tell you the truth

Or you will continue to lose every dude

It will be a sad scene as you are really a crown jewel.

Unless you change you will continue to be in your own way.

I'll just have to let the cards get played as they may as I
told you all you had to do on this wonderful day.

Easy Pt. 1
By: R.J. Edwards

I'm out here building a legacy,

It's not my fault these broads chase me.

That's why I make the game looks so easy

You know these broads out here mad sleazy

I mean easy

I mean would fuck you for some yezzy's.

I mean they just want to please me

Thinking I'd wife them

Then they could have it easy

Better yet put a baby in them

Then they know they'll stay cheesy.

From a check they'll get once a month.

All because I miss calculated the second to last pump.

Limits
By: R.J. Edwards

It's crazy how people that are in your life will
continually try to put their limitations on you.

Fear is not in my vocabulary as I wouldn't be
where I am today if I listened to fools.

Listening to you let me truly understand why you're
not doing what you want to be doing

Who do you think you're fooling?

If your dreams were in front of you on a plate you'd be drooling.

Sorry life doesn't happen that way you wish, you
have to walk through those valleys.

And those dark mysterious alleys.

To get those dreams that's farfetched and sometimes never seen.

Mountains are hard to climb but once someone conquers it.

Now everyone sees the dream.

It can be done they're now willing to rise from their hidden pit

Limits are meant to be tested and put to rest
as that's how you become the best

No one ever made history by playing it safe.

Ask Jackie Robinson, Martin Luther King, Rosa Parks and Malcolm X.

Nothing they went through was a piece of cake

All they did was keep moving and asked what's next?

Limits and boundaries are for those who want to play it safe

That's cool to know, you're not up for the race.

Inspiration
By: R.J. Edwards

I'm here to give you inspiration.

To pay you back for your suffering with love reparations.

I'm here to inspire you to be greater,

Not just a baby maker.

I'm here to help you achieve all your dreams and goals

And to fill those painful empty holes.

I'm here to help you get all that you desire,

To show you I'm not a parking meter and our time will never expire.

Let me replace that frown,

With your missing crown.

You are a Queen of royalty,

Let me show you real loyalty.

Never to take your kindness as a weakness

I will always make sure you enjoy your existence.

Your love towards me,

Is like something from a movie.

Let our love show through the way we treat each other.

Believing that death is the only way we'll cheat each other.

For when you leave, I'll be all alone.

With no one to call on the phone.

Spending my nights thinking of our memories,

Wishing they would stay with me for a thousand centuries.

I don't think you realize how much you mean to me,

You changed my forever and now there's no reaching me.

All I can do now is flee.

For without you in my life, it's just a mystery.

Keys
By R.J. Edwards

Not everyone deserves a key to your sanctuary.

For most will come and rob you of your hopes and
dreams, and then fly off like a canary.

Even though as beautiful and bright as they
were, they don't deserve that key.

As they only showed you their good side to get close to you.

Gain your respect and trust just to dismantle you.

Stealing your loving spirit that is as big as an
oak, would end up killing you.

Leaving you to live a life so meaningless and carefree.

Therefore, be mindful of who you give keys to.

To stay truly as the beautiful you.

As keys hold the power to access the wonders of the world.

Everyone doesn't deserve a key in your life, as
some want to take you just for a twirl.

Life already contains many ups and downs.

That's why the receivers should be selected and

be responsible for all those frowns.

Not everyone deserves a key.

Please, trust me.

As I used to believe I would be all I could be.

Until I trusted someone with a key that wasn't deserving of me.

Preparing a Meal
By: R.J. Edwards

Why do you read from that book?

This book, I need it to cook.

To boil in your mind life lessons,

To simmer in your mind known blessings,

To drain you of your imperfections,

To prepare you for unknown questions,

To bless you with intellect,

And to feed you pure affection to connect.

That's why I read from this book.

And I think I like the look

You Remind Me
By: R.J. Edwards

You remind me of this girl I once knew.

Gave her everything should could imagine but she still acted brand new.

I've only dealt with a chosen few,

On some knowing everything about me shit.

Who would have thought your action would
have me unwilling to commit?

It hit my heart so deep,

For even when I had a girl we used to creep.

Took you out on dates and brought you flowers.

Even though they never lasted forever.

Maybe a couple of hours.

Who would have known you would remind
me of a girl that took me for a fool?

I'm not bitter from the situation.

As she just gave me a tool

To use the next time I meet a fine chick like you.

No More
By: R.J. Edwards

You need to start elevating your mind.

You know it's not a crime no more.

It's the right thing to do, to try to even the score.

Since they can't tell you, you can't read and write no more.

You must do it as that's what our ancestors fought for.

For they can't tell you that you can't enter through this door,

As they stood up and said no more!

There is no more shackles on your hands and feet,

So, unshackle your mind and show them a different type of defeat.

Bless are those who take the high road against transgressions.

For they will see no more of the oppressor in their ascension.

They love to hate and to see us fall.

As they will be the minors and bow to our call.

Read to your eyes get tired and then read some more.

Get as much knowledge as you can to see what they fought for.

To give us a fighting chance to live right in this promise land.

And not be taken advantage of no more.

Grow into Greatness
By: R.J. Edwards

From the concrete I watched you grow.

Through the rain and the snow.

From the seasons of sunshine I watched you grow.

Even though people tried to stop you by spraying poison on you.

You shook it off and continued to glow.

The weeds were dying by your side.

Trying to tell you, you're not going to make it, so die.

You stood tall in the face of the negative talk and continued to grow.

Now that your petals have blossomed you've
shaded the others from destruction.

So, that they too can continue to grow in
amelioration and stop further castration.

Young Man
By: R.J. Edwards

Young man! Why are you walking around here showing your ass?

Acting like you were raised with no class.

When you were growing up did your parents not whoop your ass?

Now you stand on those corners smoking that gas.

Saying you know the rule cos puff puff pass.

Don't you know what people behaving like you will always end up last?

When you get older wishing you did things different in the past.

There is greatness inside of you.

But all you do to yourself is feel sorry and you want others to do that too.

I'm sorry I'm not you because I want to see you through to the other side.

Where you have a nice ride.

Big home two car garages by its side.

A life that isn't a façade.

Come take a walk with me and find out how great you can be.

For Young Man I want you to be the greatest you can be.

The Game
By: R.J. Edwards

The Game: One day you're living it up and
everyone is screaming your name.

Will have you seating in an empty basement not
even able to remember your name.

The Game: Can be a distraction from everyday life.

But in the end we'll all have to pay a price.

That we didn't see coming.

While running and gunning.

The Game: It's very unpredictable.

Can have you on the highest of the tables.

Or the lowest of lows, it's so capable.

And they won't even shed you a tear.

From all your failed dreams and broken gears.

It will keep going shouting out boos and cheers.

Now, you may not have many years in the fame and the game

But realize the joy you got when you conquered your fears and pain.

The Game: It's special without a doubt

But just know what it's about.

Get your money while you can,

As it's always gearing up for the next man.

It must keep the plan going because without it it'll fail.

And most blacks would really end up in hell.

The Game: How does it survive?

By eating our young men alive.

By making them feel invincible.

But with one slip they become replaceable.

Take a shot
R.J. Edwards

Most people go through life without ever taking a shot.

Don't they know they have to figure out what they got?

Not me though, I've taken so many shots.

I'm like Steph Curry even when he's not hot.

You're living a dream that you're not even in,

Helping others reach their goals while you're dying within.

Make a conscious decision to break the cycle of your thinking,

As it's your turn to start winning.

Raymond J. Edwards Jr
By: R.J. Edwards

Raymond James Edwards Junior is a man who
refuses to lose and does whatever he choose.

Even though as a youngster he was mentally and
sexually abused he still refused to lose.

He used to fight a lot of older guys due to his size.

But never came home with a bloody nose.

He was never despised losing to those guys as he still refused to lose.

He was always told he wouldn't be great by his family
friends and guys in the neighborhood.

He ended up doing a lot of good.

As He didn't listen to any of the sayings which were rude.

He let this fuel him and spent countless hours in gym.

Even though things always seem kind of grim.

He knew he had a lot of fight within.

He kept it going till he inked that contract with a fine pen.

Bold
By: R.J. Edwards

Why do you think you can be so bold?

Don't you know how many girls I have on hold?

I know that came off real cold,

But I thought you should know my G-Code.

Life is such a silly game and people love to play.

Most people out here are linking up with people for a quick lay.

You should have saw by my actions I wanted to be bold with you

Walking in the park holding hands with you,

Letting every chick that passes by know you are my boo.

But you choose to let your ego get the best of you.

Styling and profiling like I didn't want to see the best in you.

Instead you want to see my advances as
another poor excuse to get with you

Not knowing I was just trying to give you clues.

I wanted to be so bold with you.

So bold I wanted to make sure you said I do

I wanted to be so bold with you

That I had it in my vows to tell everyone in ear
shot that God broke the mold with you

I wanted to continue to show you that there would
never be a retraction of my feelings.

But you had other plans and a whole bunch of other dealings.

Just know my love for you would have been bold and through the ceiling.

Instead you showed me a part of you that was so unappealing.

So, it's time for me to call up another to get started on this healing.

Fear
By: R.J. Edwards

I was raised never to look up to you or live by your standards.

You are the reason many people never fulfilled their dreams.

You kept them in bondage, so you wouldn't be lonely.

You worked to make everyone bow to you like you're some
type of god, but you don't know you are really a fraud.

For when I conquered you, you crumbled beneath me.

You became a stepping stone to my destiny and a stairway for others to follow cause all your threats are very shallow.

Be All You Can Be
By: R.J. Edwards

They say no man is left behind.

But, when they come home they get to put in double time.

How is getting a couple medals going to help them shine?

When they can't even pay their rent on time.

They put their lives on the line

They come home without even earning an honesty dime.

So, how is it you are still willing to form a line?

The Star Spot
By: R.J. Edwards

Why is it that everyone wants the star spot?

Is it for everyone to know that you are hot?

That can't be it!

Because with that spot, everyone is all up in your business.

You can't even go chill with this lady or two.

Without people in your face being rude.

And if you stay in the house to yourself, then you're just a rich prude.

What is it about this spot?

Is it the money and the fame?

For without it you'd be just another lame

It's funny how people that are not in that spot have the most fun.

They don't have to run every time they see paparazzi come,

Or change their lives to a whole bunch one by one.

Life can be a little down without the money and fame.

Having that spot could also make you very lame.

Not able to really enjoy people as such.

For you don't know why they're around.

With people blowing your head up so much,

It's hard for you to see the ground.

The spot can make you lose who you are.

When you first get it, you didn't think it would go that far.

Remember to always stay humble,

For it only takes one stumble for you to tumble.

Not a Boss
By: R.J. Edwards

How do you call yourself a boss?

The only time you get money is after you've been tossed.

Nowadays people get the lines crossed.

They will be spending someone else's money like water being spilled.

Now they figure that they too are boss

How did people become so lost?

Is it because everybody's life nowadays is so false?

Make sure you live a life that allows you to be true to yourself.

Not just a pretender who could be left up collecting dust on a bookshelf.

As you can never be called oneself.

Oblivious
By: R.J. Edwards

Was I that oblivious as to why you were truly with me,

And calling me your King?

Was it all just to get a seed and a ring?

I loved you for all you were and all you would become.

But all you wanted was to make me cum.

So, you could have my child and just be a lazy bum.

Sometimes, I sit and wonder why you wanted to cause me so much pain?

Was it just to plunder my money and then walk away,

With tears pouring out of my eyes like rain?

For my heart was broken yet again.

Who knows if I'd ever endure the pain,

And try to love again?

For my love is like water getting poured down a drain.

Pouring never to remain.

I refuse to lose my love as love conquers all.

Having heirs to the throne I must love all.

And show them through it all that you must stand tall.

Thank you for another war wound round.

As my sons will see that Daddy went to battle.

And through the ups and downs,

I never let my spirit get dismantled.

Even though I was oblivious.

It was such a much bigger reason for this,

To know that angels do exist.

BEAUTY

Fly Girl
By R.J. Edwards

You got these guys out here straight drooling.

They trying to play it cool but who do they think they're fooling?

You're laughing because you know it's the truth.

For only if they could spend a night with you,

They'd jump off a roof.

Just to die a happy man,

They are ready to cut their lifespan.

You get a kick out of it too.

Speaking like Mr. Tee, "I pity the fool"

As you walk by,

Making sure to put a little more sway in your hips.

Then look back with a flip and watch as the drool drips.

You think to yourself, "ain't that a trip?"

They don't even know I'm a real bitch!

I want you to spoil me, treat me like royalty.

If you don't, I'll never show you loyalty.

You grow up rich.

All up in Beverly Hills.

Where guys always gave me expensive thrills.

But you say now that I'm older I need to chill.

We are not kids anymore, we now pay bills.

Oh yes! I'm a fly girl. I really need another guy to buy me some heels.

Your Eyes
By: R.J. Edwards

Your eyes are so beautiful when you look at me the way that you do

You make it seems as if I'm truly special to you

Like you love my simple tanned brown skin

Or that you love the way that I grin.

Can it be the way I move when I'm deep within?

Either way your eyes is so beautiful when you
look at me the way that you do

Is it because deep down you want to be my boo?

Can it be from the sight of me that I get you so
hot and bothered as if you had the flu?

Maybe you just looking at me saying boy are you
through, so it can just be me and you

Either way your eyes are so beautiful when
you look at me the way that you do.

Broken Queen
By: R.J. Edwards

You started out a young beautiful Queen from Brooklyn.

Had all the brothers on the block saying "what's up good looking?"

They didn't know that you were up in the kitchen cooking.

Working to get some bookings.

You had dumb skills with the tongue and was never second to none.

You took women's rap to the upper echelon and won.

You're still such a beautiful Queen.

But the changes that are coming was so unseen.

The face lift, butt shots, and nose jobs what did it all mean

You made it and you accomplished your dream.

Was it because you had a so-called King who
wasn't so keen on your looks?

You listen to do this dude who never picked up a history book.

The words that he said should have never bothered
you or made you want to change your look.

For you shook up the world and rewrote the rap history book.

Now, you don't have the same vibe as you wear this new disguise.

Why did you listen to those guys?

You were such a beautiful sexy Nubian Queen.

Wish I could take it back to the 90's when you looked so mean.

Cause I would get down on one knee and give you a ring.

Beauty and The Beast
By: R.J. Edwards

Could you love me?

Even if I looked like a Beast?

Love me from the east to the west.

I've showed you nothing but the best and you deserve nothing less.

Even though you know I'm a beast in these streets.

Creeping every time, I get a peek from one of these lonely freaks.

But you know it is only for one night.

For me seeing the beauty I put on your face is such a wonderful sight.

I know my two lives don't add up for what you want.

You know from the jump I was a beast and you still
fell in love with me so don't try and front.

I'll always continue to show you the beauty of me through my actions.

As long as you know the beast will show when
it comes to those sexy distractions.

The beauty in your eyes is all I see.

But you must understand that there is a beast that lives inside of me.

Two sides
By: R.J. Edwards

Pretty girls what do you do to us

I mean are you guys witches and put us under a spell

For you can put us through all kinds of hell

Everyone else sees it but we can't tell

Is it the pretty face that got us hypnotized?

Or is it those sexy hips that got us immobilized

Can it be the sex that that keeps us in a firm
grip cos boy it show is bonafide.

The way you glide down this stick and have me
mesmerized by watching the sway of your hips

Riding me so good got me stuttering and shit

Talking to me all nasty and shit

Telling me how you are my naughty, nasty and freaky little bitch

It's a damn shame to find out that's how you run game

To think I was very close to giving you my last name

I tell you

You women are slicker than a can of oil

Us men need to see more clearly the plan that you all try to uncoil

We be blinded by the looks you see

Being called the man if we bag thee and can call her wifey

See that's the spell that keeps most of us in hell

Worrying about the outside world and how those hips twirl

Instead of if she's really that wonder girl

Who can truly change your world and make your toes curl

Make you not ever want to look at another girl

Make your life stress free

Let you be

Make you want to grind to make her happy cause
she keeps you with a peace of mind

She also loves it from behind

Makes you breakfast lunch and dinner every day without complaining

Do you get what I'm saying?

This is the woman worth living for daily

She ain't lazy

Takes care of the babies

Let everyone knows she's your lady

While handling everything smoothly like gravy

There's is no better lady

Fight those temptations and spells

Or spend the rest of your days in a living hell

Best Friend
By: R.J. Edwards

I met you in a city called Cincinnati.

You were so beautiful when you walk through those school doors,

Filling those corridors with a fragrance that smelled so scintillatingly.

Having every girl looking to see how they could even the score.

You brought about change in many ways,

All those girls should thank you till this day.

I know you used to hate it when I asked where your mama is.

But you knew I was just joking as I didn't want to start no drama

As it was you I truly wanted to see.

But, our friendship meant more to me.

So, me and you couldn't be.

HATRED

Jealousy
By: R.J. Edwards

You fill people with so much envy and hate
towards those that want to be great.

We all get the same twenty-four hours.

Why are you mad at me for using mine the right
way and not sleeping in bed late?

I get up and grind everyday so no one else can tell me my fate.

It's in my own hands because I want to be great.

Not just for myself but for my family, friends and community.

So why are you always trying to trip me up and start a mutiny?

There is truly no real difference between you and me!

Besides the fact that I'm willing to put in the work to my soul hurts

But I forgot your name is jealousy.

That's your claim to fame.

Bringing the next man down because of your shame.

Damn
By: R.J. Edwards

You'll be missed

Sike I lied

We don't care about you in this bitch

We could have found you somewhere dead in a
ditch and still wouldn't have given a shit.

For all the foul shit you made us go through

Never being there for Birthdays

Or after we fell and hurt ourselves and telling us it would be ok

It'll be fourteen years soon that I haven't seen you face to face.

Just know when I do see you I have a lot of shit to say

I hope it ain't on your death bed

Cos the shit I'm going to say might send your ass into a code red.

I don't want that shit on my conscious.

Even though subconsciously

You'll be getting what you deserve

For you were a fucked-up Father throwing your kids out on the curb

Damn you helped make us ain't that absurd

So, why you think if I see you I wouldn't look at you like a turd.

Some shit I need to flush down the toilet.

For you thought you were a Father because the government forced you to open your wallet.

TIME

No Tomorrow
By: R.J. Edwards

None of us can escape death.

Sooner or later we will see that day.

Be it as it may, don't regret today.

Live your life.

For not a day on this earth is safe.

You must move about so brave.

Don't fear anything.

Before you know it you'll be looking down on your grave.

Wondering where the time went.

As you are now seeping through the hole like air in a vent.

Time
By: R.J. Edwards

It's a quarter to noon and the sun is shining through the window

Nobody knows not even you that the night has turned you into a widow.

How's that for a change of time?

For you thought you'd have your man for a lifetime.

But you put your phone on silent after the
argument and he called you for a lifeline.

How long are you going to regret telling him he can't get out?

For he was your spouse and you thought you
were just putting him on a little timeout

Not even knowing that y'alls time had run out.

Now you are sitting there crying your eyes
out because of your selfish doubt.

And the man that you loved is laid out.

Those tears won't add years to all the things y'all dreamed about

Now you thinking to yourself if only I didn't doubt

I'd have my man here in the house

But as my luck would have it I'm left without a spouse.

For our time together has run out.

Pass
By: R.J. Edwards

We let it pass us by as if we were standing still.

The love we've been looking for was right there for our touch.

But we rather play games instead of living a life
that was built on something real.

Misjudging the facts on something that most
would kill for has us feeling so ill.

Wishing there was a pill to take that would send us back to that yesterday.

Unfortunately, we must live with this mistake for our tomorrow is today.

We've grown apart, which wasn't too smart.

For we've gotten with others and even broken their hearts.

We should have finished what we started.

Now, we gonna live the rest of our lives broken hearted.

UNITY

Unity
By: R.J. Edwards

People out here screaming unity

But your own people out steady aiming at your
head wanting you to see the holy trinity

They ain't trying to stop the violence

They just making a lot of noise just to get an audience

To pretend to drop some knowledge on your next of
kin, so they don't go out and commit a sin.

Let's show them some unity and take some of their people

Yeah that'll show them that we're lethal

For there is strength in numbers

As we can't conquer anything along.

See what Caesar did with Rome.

Don't go running home when you get punched in the face.

Unless it's to go get your brother and you all
are ready to put danger in its place

Unity is about sticking together for the common goal.

Let us be about that for greatness can return to our
neighborhood as that is the ultimate goal.

Unity

R.J. Edwards
We must come together.

To bring about peace.

Push out hate and envy.

Strangle jealousy and greed.

Show love to all.

Even those who has fallen from grace and their call.

Let's uplift their spirits so the angels can hear it,

Eliminate the strife between each other to be fit.

For we can become one

And be there for one another

Family just from another mother.

Time
By: R.J. Edwards

I love the pleasure of undressing you.

Bringing your body close to mine as I caress you.

You don't know how this is such a dream come true.

I would have held my breath till my face turned
blue just to receive a kiss from you.

I knew you were something special from the first time I met you.

You were dressed in street clothes and still had a brother on his toes

Having me wanting to smell every scent of your fragrance.

But I knew I couldn't show my impatience at that instance.

For you weren't a normal girl.

You were well reserved like a woman's pearls

In time I knew I could make you mine

I knew it would be a grind

As all amazing things take work and time

ROMANCE

Kisses
By: R.J. Edwards

Those sweet kisses, how I miss them.

How you would just kiss me on a whelm?

Never, no special occasion.

For you to place those lovely lips upon me.

I wish I had all the money in the world, so
you wouldn't have to work so hard.

I know I know you always tell me son we were dealt these cards.

But it's not fair.

Our lives shouldn't just be up in the air.

One day I'm going to be a star

Take us to place that is so far

People going to think we traveled to Mars

I became that star.

I always told you I would be

It's just so sad you're not here with me

I'll always remember those sweet kisses

For every night I say a few wishes like when I was a kid doing the dishes.

Reminiscing on how you would come by me and give me a few little kisses

Would Be Nice
By: R.J. Edwards

Come here and lay with me and her and you both share a
place on my chest while you both get your beauty rest

Don't stress about what society may think about our situation
for us coming together is the beginning of something great

Let's make no mistake it's going to be work for all of us to stay the course.

As the life we live distorts society's way of living such.

It would only bother me if I gave any fucks

I just hope that you two don't care as much.

I hope people's bad talk won't get to you and
put a strain on our relationship

Cos, I'll be down in the slumps if their negative
thoughts and views cause you to jump ship

Who says the way that other's live is the right and only way

I thought the only thing that matters is that I
can make your day, day after day.

Making you smile, laugh and feel pure joy

Knowing that my love is not fake and a ploy

I'm here to treat your heart and love like a brand-new toy

As being loved, being understood and cared for is all anyone can truly ask.

As anything else is just icing on the cake

So, don't make any mistake I'm here to build something greater
than great with two Queens that will change history to date.

Now, that our unit is formed we can handle any storm.

As we hold each other hands until a new nation is born

I pledge to you both never to leave your hearts torn.

Nice Guy
By: R.J. Edwards

You're beautiful and sexy what do I have to do to get you next to me

To bring out the best and give you all the rest of me

Give me the test so I can show you I'm better than the rest

It's no contest as I'll wash you from head to toe

Make runs to the store

Tape your favorite shows

Won't entertain these hoes.

Give you more D than you ask for

Kiss it nice and long so I won't make it sore

Surprise you with flowers and so much more

You still don't want me to be your man

Well damn I feel sorry for the next man because he doesn't stand a chance.

Embrace
By: R.J. Edwards

Let's embrace each other.

Escape in each other's arms without leaving our home.

Connecting on a higher level.

Making us feel as if we're in this world alone.

Let peace be our soap to help us become anew.

Let love shower us and wash away all our fears.

Let happiness be our towel to dry us from any tears.

Let us embrace once more for us to celebrate this
special day as we hear all the cheers.

Know that nothing in this life is going to be perfect

But I do know that with us by each other's side there is nothing to fear.

Can I
By: R.J. Edwards

Can I hold you,

All through the night?

Till we see daylight

I'd be fine if it's only

For One Night.

WORDS FOR HER

Unconditional
By: R.J. Edwards

When she looks at me all she sees is a blank face.

It's not because I'm emotionless and it's not because I fear this

I just know all that I've put you through you don't deserve this.

I just wonder how this could be

That you would show me so much mercy

You really meant it when you said our life together would be a journey.

Lost Two
By: R.J. Edwards

I'm sorry my life's journey has created something
in me that you can't endure

Know there is no one that I adore more

You are so beautiful, sexy, strong and powerful

Any man will be lucky to have you by his side for his final hour.

For he would know he couldn't have seen any better
days except looking into your wonderful gaze

I know that day will come where you will have to move on from me

Just know I'll always love you till my head turn into a head full of grays.

You Mad
By: R.J. Edwards

Are you mad that I'm cut from a different cloth than you?

That I can put myself in a situation same as you

But, the difference between me and you I know
not to catch those feelings booboo.

It's okay that you're not built like me

But don't try and hold that against me

We were supposed to be cooler than those three musketeers

Now, you are hoping and wishing that I'm going
to call you with a fist full of tears.

Girl bye, you know how many years that pasted since
my eyes has seen tears over the opposite sex

Think about it why would I cry over someone
who wouldn't even be considered an ex.

I'm just cut from a different cloth

I'm not the moth.

I'm the flame

You need to remember my name.

Cherry
By: R.J. Edwards

Your womb is where I love to be.

The pleasure zone till the end of eternity.

Brings me peace no matter what the world is trying to do to me.

I promise to take care of it carefully.

For you put the cherry on my life so perfectly.

Wonder
By: R.J. Edwards

You wonder why it can't be just you and me

How come you're not enough for me?

How come I like to have two or three?

It is very simple you're just not enough

Sorry I just had to be blunt

It's time to be real with this stuff

You said I've been like a breath of fresh air

So, is it fair to me knowing you don't truly satisfy me?

Now, can you see why I need two or three?

For when I ask you to do certain things you
give me this look of uncertainty

As you don't know how to do what I just asked thee

You knew when you met me I was an unusual human being

Knowing you'd be asked to do things you couldn't
even imagine in your wildest dreams

We're old enough where I shouldn't have to be doing all this teaching

I know you wonder to yourself how he can say he loves me
when he knows he needs more to even out our score

I hope this lets you know why you should wonder no more

Black Queen
By: R.J. Edwards

You are always talking about how you keep your
head held high despite any adversity

So, why when posing for a picture you're quick to bow your head.

Like you are ashamed of what might be seen in whatever city

I know people can be mean and quick to judge

You know better than anyone else to get to the
top you must walk through some sludge

Especially after so many tries of them trying to
run your name through the mud.

So, please keep your head held high and blind
all the haters with that beautiful smile
For a man like me it'll help me go that extra mile.

What If
R.J. Edwards

What if I would have made you my lady
instead of my first of many mistakes
Would you and I have been greater than red velvet cupcakes
Did we have the love it would have taken to last through all the hating
Let's not forget about all the judgment that would have come our way
For I still remember that day
When you ran and hid on our way to the movies
I thought you were just playing
You could have fooled me
But you kept it all the way real
That you couldn't get caught with me
If you did you'd have to plea your case
Moreover, we were just beginning our race
I understood your logic and accepted it
But I think my conscious kept a hold of it
For when it came time for me to decide I'd always picked
the latter for I knew with you I'd have to be a secret and
keep my mouth shut about my favorite crush
Someone that I loved and cherished I wouldn't have been
able to hold in public till we were bonded by marriage
I guess I was selfish and that what put a strain on what
could have place us in a horse and carriage

For now, through the space and time

I can see it would have been a remarkable thing to call you mine

Unknown
By: R.J. Edwards

You wonder why I do what I do.

You ask too.

Not knowing,

You still won't get the answer that you are looking for.

Stop asking because you will never even out the score.

I Knew
By: R.J. Edwards

It's funny how time flies.

From the first day I saw that twinkle in your eyes

I never felt that way before seeing such beauty standing in the door

Long hair, gorgeous face, beautiful smile, lovely body with amazing style

Oh, how I wonder how you would look coming down an aisle

With that, being said, I had to approach with a smile.

Being Your Best
By: R.J. Edwards

Baby let me show what I can do when I put this tool on you

See look at you about to get an attitude

Because you thought I was talking about what is
between my legs and how I could use it on you

Instead I was talking about my other head and
how I can show you chivalry ain't dead.

Nor are romantic gestures a thing of the past

I'm sorry your last man didn't show you and
was always looking to show his ass

Just know that's a thing of the past for on you I'll spend my last.

To show you it is you I truly adore

You better not touch that door

I'm here to show you how a true King treats his Queen

As you see I didn't tell you but show you.

As actions speak louder than words

My love for you needs to be seen

For the world can know I love My Queen

No, babe I'm not doing it to mean.

Other Queens need to know that their Kings need to have them.

Feel like they are living in a dream.

For life without you would be meaningless

My goal in this life is to show you I'm not useless.

The User
By: R.J. Edwards

I want you to know that I'm not your type

I'm going to do a whole bunch of shit you don't like

I'm not going to text you every night

Nor, will I be paying for you to take a flight.

I'm not the caring type

I just want you to come over, so I can lay this pipe

Call you an uber and say goodnight

Don't text when you get home safe.

That booty was just alright,

Only time I'll hit you again is if it's a super late night.

Special
By: R.J. Edwards

Since you walked into my life you've been nothing short of real

I wish I could have known how you truly felt about me

Because I would have close the deal

You could have already been My Fifi.

Our connection was never lost as we always stayed in touch

For I know deep down inside we always had a crush

We let many years pass as we both dealt with a lot of trash

You don't know how happy I am to say that's all now in the past.

For I've come clean to you about my feelings

You confirmed to me letting me know that you are willing

To explore all these wonderful amazing feelings for one another

I want to show you how my love is smooth like butter.

Making you smile on a daily basis

Makes me feel like I'm covering all the bases

Hence the smile I have as I look into your eyes

Letting you know there will be no more goodbyes.

Understand
By: R.J. Edwards

I know times right now is a little bit rough.

Just know I'm here to help you get through this tough stretch.

I'll never turn my back on you in this dark moment.

You were always there to give me my atonement.

Life is full of peaks and valleys.

Very dark alleys.

But, knowing there is a light at the end of the tunnel,

Allows your eyes to make a funnel.

To focus only on that light of hope.

Moreover, I'm still here the same because I think you are so dope.

As my love for you is more than skin deep.

If I had to work ten jobs, I'll do it to make sure that we eat.

Know that you're never a burden and I'll never
close the curtain on our love.

To me it is as pure as a dove.

The Truth
By: R.J. Edwards

I'm always here for the deep conversations

Any inquisitive questions

I am an open book

But like a worm you got to put me on the hook

If you want to catch a gigantic fish

And to have him preparing you your special dish

You must want to get to know him

If you want him to want to get to know you

That's the part need it in both of you convincing
each other why we should be boos

How would that have happened if you didn't
ask questions and get the clues

On what makes each other happy and sad

You most definitely need to know what makes each other mad

Ask the questions you need before you wish you had

Myth

By: R.J. Edwards

I'm the Myth your mother warned you about

I'm the one who was born to make you doubt
everything your mother ever told you about

I'm the one who will have you breaking all the rules

Teaching you things you can't learn in schools.

I'm the one who will never give you the blues

Nor having you look like a fool as most thinks that is cool

I'm the one who is going to tell you the truth no matter how much it hurts

As I'm not an inconsiderate jerk.

I'm not into taking someone's feelings lightly, I want to
make sure our love is pure and off the chart.

How do I expect that to happen with a broken heart?

I'm the one who will have you doing things you never thought you'd do.

Like, skinny dipping in the pool and having sex in the jacuzzi too.

I'm the one who you get married to

As you know life will be an adventure

That you'll never be down and blue.

Our love will also be front and center too.

For I just don't know what I'll do without you

Let's turn our lives into a joint venture

Hibernating all of December.

It's
By: R.J. Edwards

It's amazing what a couple of words can do

Think about it.

How do you feel when someone tells you, "I love you"?

Does your heart not just melt?

It's a special feeling that you feel

It's like they've healed all your wounds

From your past of those stupid buffoons

It's amazing what a couple of words can do.

Think about it

When someone gets on one knee and ask, "will you marry me?"

How wonderful would you feel?

That someone feels that they have found all they needed in you.

You say, "yes" because you've found all you needed too.

Never take for granted what words can do as they

can make someone feel high or low.

Untitled
R.J. Edwards

I'm sorry that I fell in love with two.

Because I don't know what I would do without the both of you

Let's do like before they got on a boat

Because neither of us deserves to have our heart broke.

I know rules say that you can't have two but why
should their rules apply to me, you and you.
People always say two is better than one but
just imagine what three could do
A King and Two Queens
There is no limit in what we could do.
As there is strength in numbers and you my Queens is greatest amongst us
I don't know if this journey will ever begin.
If it does I'll do everything in my power to make sure it doesn't end

Please Explain
By: R.J. Edwards

How you talking boss shit when you are just a runner
Bosses do Boss shit
All you do is talk shit.
About what you gonna do.
When in life you ain't even got a clue
Where your next meal is coming from
Cause you get fed from the next man hand
Back in the day we called you a J.A.B.A.N
Just a Bitch Ass Nigga.

Repayment
By: R.J. Edwards

Truly there's no me without you
I was in the dark and you saw me through.
You were my light at the end of the tunnel

Without you my life would have crumbled.

Just know you've awaken another beast in me

Now, I am working to give you everything you deserve times three.

Listen
By: R.J. Edwards

I'm the man of your dreams and everything in between

I shine like a diamond now

But can you understand what I went through to get here

Are you willing to listen with both ears?

No, I mean really listen

Not just listen to give a reply

To listen to make sure I'm really that guy

The guy of your dreams, desires and fantasies

Not just another guy trying to get what's in your panties

Listen up closely to the things I'm about to say

For it should determine if you would want to leave or stay

BETRAYAL

How Could You
By: R.J. Edwards

You told me you loved me, but you lied to me

Where did I go wrong in loving you?

You asked for it and I gave it

If you didn't have it, I went to get it

You told me you loved me, but you lied to me

How could you hurt me?

When you know I would have given you my last?

I was even ok with you sometimes showing your ass

Not once did I bring up your crazy past

But you still chose to lie to me

Why would you set out to hurt me?

The pain you caused, that'll never leave me

Why would you leave a stain on me?

True Colors
By: R.J. Edwards

Even when I had trust issues I trusted you

From our long talks I know you had been used and abused too

I thought that would have brought us closer

Except you turned around and used everything I told you against me

Knowing it was going to cause me more pain and agony

I felt like nothing when your true intentions surfaced

How didn't I see how you was so phony and two faced

I should have realized that was what you were

from telling me about you close friends

Who had more than one man and had a husband

I should have known you were trifling

For all you look for is causing strife

I listened to you when you said you'd be a great wife

Break Away
By: R.J. Edwards

I had trust issues before I met you

Now they even worst after you

Sike I lied

Well not about the trust issues yeah those are true

But everything got better since you

Not having to prove I was truly only in to you and how
I was out here not trying to screw other broads

It's such a monkey off my back

I know if I would have been with you for life
I would have had a heart attack

You would have been constantly stressing
and testing me to the third degree

Instead of just letting me be

A faithful and loving man

Who's always willing to work for the upper hand.

Showering my love ones with trips to the mall to spend a couple of grand

But you on the other hand didn't see that at all

All you saw was a way for you to implement your evil plan

Not knowing it will be the last time I would take stand

I was able to peel the wool off my eyes and
really saw where your spirit truly lies

Now we have no ties and it's just me and my guys

Is It
By: R.J. Edwards

Why is it so how hard for me to get the attention I deserve from you?

I give you everything you ask for and more.

You want for nothing.

Is it so hard for you to even the score?

I get you fresh flowers on a weekly basis

Buy you wine by the cases

Why is it that I must beg for some attention?

Must I mention the five carat I bought for you for our engagement?

I never lied to you about making your dreams come true.

Why is it you treat me the way that you do?

For I worship the ground that you walk on.

Never have I failed you by leading another on.

My eyes are and have always been just for you.

You can't tell from the way I shower you.

Why is it now that you're crying that sad song?

As your actions showed that you did no wrong.

You acted as if everything I did was just for show.

You see me doing it for another that's what
is really making your heart sore

Cause she is appreciating what you were receiving and more.

Why must it take losing someone for you to
know you had really hit the big score?

Who Knew?
By: R.J. Edwards

Who knew that after your last relationship
that your heart would went cold.

I just thought it was a chapter that was written
in a story that would be told.

But you felt betrayed and let down.

You built walls as high as the highest mountains
and they wasn't coming down.

For no one could ever pierce your heart.

Hit you with that line, oh let's be friends.

Knowing damn well they are going to try and stick it in.

Get you addicted to what you've been missing without
giving you what you've been wishing.

That is a man full of commitment.

That knows how to get it.

That knows you're his golden ticket to all he has been missing.

That you are His Queen not just something to get in between.

You are the Rock to his foundation.

He knows there's no replacing you for you know it too

Who knew that I would change you and you
would so do the same for me too.

Missed Out
R.J. Edwards

You had me under lock and key

But you chose to try and destroy me

Who knew what we had wasn't real

For I was willing to kill to show you it was real.

Guess the things I was giving you like love, attention,
affection and understanding didn't fuel you

I'm glad I know it was you

That didn't deserve what I was giving you.

For my expression was to always drown you in love

Knowing I'd place no one else above

Life is full of a lot of uncertainty.

So, how on earth do you throw love away not
knowing if that love will ever be replaced?

Now, you are just all by yourself staring into space
and my love is gone now without a trace.

Memories are faded.

Pictures are out dated.

Bet you didn't know from that point on your love would be tainted

Wasted Love
R.J. Edwards

I bet you're wishing you can hit the reset

To get yourself out of your love debt.

Cos, now your love is just spent

Going in all the wrong directions

Remember when you didn't have to use discretion

Now you got to creep from hotel to hotel not
knowing who's going to try and tell.

Who knew the love you had would fail due to your faulty actions

Thinking they wouldn't have any reaction.

Now you about to be on some real fatal attraction type of shit

Then you going to get the labeled that crazy bitch

Putting your love deeper in a ditch

Having you wish there was a real-life Hitch.

Taker
By: R.J. Edwards

It just sounds nice to you calling me bae or boo.

I figured out the reason you do.

It's all about what I can do for you.

Who would have thought.

You were all about yourself.

To think I thought you were top shelf.

Thought I had a winner.

Turned out you were just with me because my bread was bigger.

And longer than the next go getter.

Selfish
By: R.J. Edwards

The only thing that matters to you.

Is if I keep a smile on your face.

If I don't you'd look at me in disgrace.

I wonder how you can do that, maybe by grace.

When you say being with me,

Is your happy place.

I know what it is.

You are just my mistake.

All you do is look to take.

When all I wanted us to do is be great and not be fake.

Disturbed
By: R.J. Edwards

Why would you turn me down for such a clown?

Was it because you thought I'll always be around?

Did I show you too much interest?

Was it because you knew I would be your

Manstress if you would have let me.

No, that can't be.

You just wanted to continue to take me for granted.

You knew I was distracted by your beauty.

Or better yet mesmerized by your beauty.

For on this Earth I've never seen a beauty such as yourself.

Most people would think I'm just talking about your beauty.

Which is not the case for your brain and spirit is just as beautiful.

If not more I'm just sad that I truly didn't get to explore your inner depths

And take it to that next step.

For that pain and agony, the next time you come around.

I might just feel like turning you down.

As you played me like a clown and spent me like a merry-go- round.

I know now that beauty skin deep is shallow like a pond.

There's no chance of us forming a bond.

As still waters run deep.

Sadly, you're no deeper than a creek.

News
By: R.J. Edwards

I'm sitting here with a puzzled look on my face as I received this news.

How could you do this to me sleeping around
town on me with other dudes?

Did you figure you had nothing to lose?

That all I would do was go around singing the blues.

Don't you remember I ain't wrapped so tight?

So now it's going to be a lot of fights on the list tonight.

As they all knew you were mine.

And they crossed that line.

That you don't cross when other man plants
a flag on other man's fertile land.

For now, they all must catch these hands.

Because they have ruined my plans to take you to mother-land.

Blessing me with some precious babies,

And putting you up in a sweet Mercedes and calling you my old lady.

Breakup
By: R.J. Edwards

I don't mind being that man in your corner.

But, you leave me for months on end with a boner.

Please, know someone is going to come keep me warmer

That's why I'll rather be a loner.

I'm no one's property

I'm sorry if you doubted me.

Should I say doubted because I told you what I needed?

You just choose to be conceited.

Now you are the one sitting there feeling cheated.

Time Is Up
By: R.J. Edwards

Now that my attention is purely focused on me.

Now you want to try and focus on me.

How does that work?

For when I asked for attention you gave me the cold shoulder.

Now you got to carry around that regret boulder.

I don't give cold threats.

I just move on to what's next.

How do you get me back?

It's on to the next for the both of us.

For moving on is an absolute must.

As there is no more love not even lust.

Fake Friends
By: R.J. Edwards

Watch who you call your friend!

The snake can be seating right at home.

Waiting for the right time to bust you in the dome.

Either with the chrome.

Be careful not to spread yourself thin.

Not hanging with the right person,

Will have you spending days in the state pen.

Straight No Chaser
By: R.J. Edwards

I know where I went wrong

I shouldn't have cared at all

Seeing what you could be was my downfall

How we could've had everything and showed everybody else how to ball

All you wanted was a reason to get what you get every first of the month

Which was straight dumb

You could have had all that and more

Now all you get to see is what I had in store

A life full of love, happiness and joy

Now only thing you get is to play with your toy

Maybe that's just it

You knew you weren't shit so you sabotage our relationship

You know you could have saved me a lot of time and money
if you just would have been real with your shit

Now all I see is a selfish, lying, conniving and manipulating witch.

Human Beings
By: R.J. Edwards

I want real-ships not relationships.

Why can't people get with this.

It's so simple, just be real.

Like what is the deal.

No one seems to tell the truth.

How are you suppose to rock with someone and get into a groove,

And make sure that y'alls flower bloom.

When you know all people do is lie and look to fuck over you.

Guess you have to deal with people to you figure
out who is really down for you.

FORGIVENESS
AND RECONCILATION

Please Forgive Me
By: R.J. Edwards

I know I cheated on you

I know you thinking I must have lost my mind

I know damn well you're a dime and ain't here to be played

I also know you love me enough to stay

There is no way for me to make this up to you but know
every day of my life I'll never stop trying too

You are the glue to our family I know I messed up and you can't stand it

Please allow me to stay in your life and don't make me out to be a bandit

Life is full of lessons

Let this be that

I promise I won't make it into regret

Another woman will never be a threat

Ups and Downs
By: R.J. Edwards

It's funny how you're trying to pick up the pace.

Where was this effort when I needed that warm embrace?

Now that I'm about to leave you want to give chase.

It's crazy that we've even gotten to this place.

There wasn't a day that went by that you didn't have me lit like a fireplace.

Now I barely even get to see your face.

I want you and you also want me.

How do we get back to our happy place.

RESPECT AND LOYALTY

Respect Me
By: R.J. Edwards

Respect me enough not to fear me

Allow me to show you ways to grow into something different

Which allows you to show me undeniable loyalty.

For if you fear me the respect can and will fade

As you will get tired of living in that shade of my shadow

From here the plot thickens as you look to close the reign of my rule

We all can say that there is a new rule it's
better to be respected than feared

For, if you are feared sooner or later the people who
love you their eyes will be filled with tears

As they have suffered over many years because of the fear

Spread love and happiness and watch the respect come

Ruling like a tyrant is sure to leave you with none

Loyalty
By: R.J. Edwards

I never knew if anyone really had my back

Do you know how that feels?

Thinking about it is making me feel ill.

How could this be?

When I'm filled with nothing but loyalty.

Shouldn't I be treated like royalty?

Nowadays you can't find a pot like that of a gold.

This being nice shit is getting old.

That's how the story unfolds.

In a warm heart turning so cold.

Just
By: R.J. Edwards

I'm just trying to see you smile for more than a while.

For I know your heart's been through it's fair share of frowns.

From all those guys that let you down.

And those that was straight clowns.

I want to be your ticket,

Showing you life has no limits.

As long as you're willing to live life in our lane.

Because if all goes well you'll have my last name.

I do wonder, could you truly accept me with all my imperfections.

Without always having a crazy number of questions.

Like who you are always texting.

And why are you always out with your boys flexing.

All I want to do is put a smile on your face.

And from time to time I'd like a little space to spread my wings

To move around town and chill with the fellas.

Just know ain't nothing these other women can
tell me for I've found My Queen

Losing you I don't even want to feel that sting.

I'm always going to be on my best behavior

Because you are my favorite flavor.

And with you by my side we are going to do things major.

For all I ever want to do is just see you smile.

Dedication

John Sr. and LeVonia Beamon

Raymond Sr. and Pauletta Edwards

John Beamon Jr.

Latricia Edwards

Bruce and Erin Hopkins

Ed Jackson

Dennis Bettis

Mike Brown

Scott And Julie Vondahaar

Jim Leon

Officer Hamler

Ernest Morgan

Mrs. Carr

Michelle Rankine

Eric Thomas

Les Brown

Zig Ziglar